*"Stephanie Chandler has done something very important: authored a book that **should be mandatory reading for entrepreneurs**. She goes way beyond the other books about success in individual enterprise because her book is chock full of both rare wisdom and precious resources. Because she asks all the right questions, her book is also loaded with right answers. Billions of people will make zillions of mistakes as entrepreneurs, but not those who have read Stephanie's 'The Business Startup Checklist and Planning Guide.'"*

-**Jay Conrad Levinson**, The Father of Guerrilla Marketing & author of the "Guerrilla Marketing" series of books, Over 14 million sold; now in 41 languages.

*"**Stephanie has created a valuable small business guide for anyone who wants to achieve greater success**. 'The Business Startup Checklist and Planning Guide's' practical exercises and sensible tactics enable people to launch and grow their dream businesses. It solves age-old challenges with real, how-to solutions and guidance."*

-**Romanus Wolter**, The Kick Start Guy and author of "Kick Start Your Dream Business" and "Kick Start Your Success." As Entrepreneur Magazine's Success Coach, radio host and speaker, he has inspired millions of people to close the gap between their goals and success. Discover more at www.kickstartguy. com.

*"The rewards of self-employment are so great that I can't imagine why everyone doesn't work for themselves. If that's a dream you have, wait no longer. Recovering corporate employee Stephanie Chandler has made the transition to the joyfully jobless life and now she's created the ultimate road map so you can follow in her footsteps. **This is the kind of information I wish I'd had when I was starting out**."*

-**Barbara J. Winter**, co-founder of the Dreambuilders Community and author "Making a Living Without a Job" and "Jumpstart Your Entrepreneurial Spirit."

*"Got questions? Get answers from Stephanie Chandler's new book, 'The Business Startup Checklist and Planning Guide: Seize Your Entrepreneurial Dreams!' **Definitely one of the most enjoyable "how-to" business books I've seen—and I've seen many!** As Stephanie and the entrepreneurs she interviews describe how they dealt with their business apprehensions and obstacles, you'll glean ideas you can apply to your own entrepreneurial quest. Plus, Stephanie gives you specific practical tools to take the guesswork out of starting a business."*

-**Francie Marks Ward**, Chief Entrepreneurial Officer & founder of Business Owners Idea Cafe, the popular spot where entrepreneurs find "A Fun Approach to Serious Business" at www.ideacafe.com.

Ten Great Reasons to Become an Entrepreneur

1. You will no longer work for someone you only pretend to like.
2. You make the rules which means you can break them whenever you want.
3. You can call yourself whatever you like: President, CEO, Founder, or COE (Chief of Everything).
4. You decide what your expense account includes.
5. You can work at home in your pajamas with your pet at your side (or on your lap, desk, etc.).
6. You can take all the long lunches you want.
7. You will be the envy of all your friends who are still stuck in jobs they hate.
8. Nobody can make you sit in another boring meeting.
9. You will control your own destiny.
10. The only pink slip you'll ever have to worry about is a phone message.

The Business Startup Checklist and Planning Guide

The Business Startup Checklist and Planning Guide

Seize Your Entrepreneurial Dreams!

By Stephanie Chandler
www.BusinessInfoGuide.com

Aventine Press

Published by Aventine Press
1023 4th Ave #204
San Diego CA, 92101
www.aventinepress.com

ISBN: 1-59330-300-9

Library of Congress Control Number: 2005930097
Library of Congress Cataloging-in-Publication Data
Chandler, Stephanie
The business startup checklist and planning guide: seize your
entrepreneurial dreams/Stephanie Chandler p. cm. Includes index
1. Business—United States. 2. Small business—Entrepreneurship 3.
Business—Home business I. Title.

Printed in the United States of America

Table of Contents

Introduction

There was a lot I wasn't prepared for when I ventured into life as an entrepreneur. Many of the challenges are topics covered in the pages of this book—an effort to help you avoid the same frustrations. Perhaps the greatest surprise has been discovering how much I enjoy this independent lifestyle. It's not like life in corporate America where I couldn't wait for the weekend. Business ownership has become a passion that consumes me.

I can't get enough of it. I want to read and absorb every bit of new information I can find on the subjects of running a business, growing profits, marketing, and being successful. I want to talk to other business owners, discover what makes them tick, and find out what works and what doesn't work for them. I want to get inside their heads.

I surf websites, subscribe to countless newsletters and e-zines, and devour books and magazines. I participate in forums, attend networking meetings, form partnerships with interesting entrepreneurs, and love to talk shop. I write articles and keep a journal on my desk filled with ideas—ideas I generate so fast that I can barely keep up with them. I even keep a notepad next to my bed so I can jot down random thoughts in the middle of the night.

I can't sleep until I've checked e-mail one last time. Of course I enjoy family time in the evenings, but when everyone leaves the room, even if for just a few minutes, I feel compelled to slip into my home office and check e-mail, view my web statistics, or submit a quick article. Living the entrepreneurial life is one filled with joys and rewards—and a bit of obsession.

Why This Book?

Toni Morrison once said, "If there is a book you really want to read but it hasn't been written yet, then you must write it." I took this advice to heart.

When I decided to depart from corporate America after more than a decade in the Silicon Valley, I spent a year and a half researching my first business (Book Lovers Bookstore in Sacramento, CA). I read dozens of business books and was frustrated by the fact that I still had questions, even after reading hundreds of pages. None of the books provided me with real resources or the nuts and bolts I needed to start a business.

I wanted to know how to find my trade associations. I wanted to know how to locate vendors and understand what their expectations would be of me. I wanted to find creative ways to market my business. I wanted to avoid surprises and prepare myself for every possibility. I wanted to know how to negotiate a lease, apply for business licenses and why I needed liability insurance. I wanted to understand the pitfalls, the fear, and the rewards of business ownership. I wanted to know how other people abandoned steady paychecks and survived. I wanted a lot of information and had to find much of it on my own.

There were some lessons I learned the hard way. For example, I set out to negotiate a commercial lease myself. Armed with a background in software sales and years of negotiation experience, I was sure I was ready to tackle the challenge. But I didn't understand much of the terminology in the contracts and quickly realized that I needed an experienced agent on my side who did.

I was still able to use my negotiation skills. In fact, I requested changes to my lease agreement that my agent didn't think would fly. "They'll never agree to a shorter lease term," she said, "and there's no way they will give you a whole year at half-rent." I had her ask anyway. We went back and forth through at least a dozen revisions. I asked for clarification of terms I didn't understand, and changes to terms I didn't agree with. When all was said and done, the majority of my requests were granted. I got the entire first year at half-rent and a variety of other concessions. The lesson learned: ask for help when you need it and trust your gut instincts.

I invested hundreds of hours researching every aspect of running a business. I was giving up a solid career and wanted to minimize the risk as much as possible by being prepared for every hurdle that I would face. I kept careful records, cataloged my resources and experiences and knew that eventually I would use my knowledge to help others do exactly what I did: kick-start their entrepreneurial dreams.

First I launched a website for entrepreneurs: www. BusinessInfoGuide.com. I wanted to provide industry-specific information for people who wanted to start businesses in retail, food and beverage, publishing, cleaning, health and fitness, and other industries. This is the kind of information I wish I had access to when I started. The site has grown rapidly to include hundreds of resources for starting and running a business along with a newsletter that I thoroughly enjoy putting together each month.

At the same time I started outlining this book. I've filled the pages with answers to the questions that I had when I started, along with actual sources that I used to find the answers I needed. You should find resources to answer virtually all of your questions about starting a business within the pages of this book. And if you don't, I want to hear about it so I can make sure to add it to the next volume.

It shouldn't be as hard or as scary as we think it is to start a business. If you have entrepreneurial instincts, are driven toward success and want to own your destiny, there is a world of opportunity waiting for you. My goal here is to make the road you travel as smooth as possible, to fill in the pot holes and unclog the crowded highway of information. And most of all, to save you a lot of time along the way.

Entrepreneur Profiles

Each chapter concludes with the profile of a successful entrepreneur. I found people all over the U.S. and Canada who were willing to share their stories: the glory and the hardships, the lessons learned, and the resources that they used to get where they are today. I think you'll agree that these are some very impressive business owners.

The entrepreneurs I have interviewed over the years own businesses in all kinds of industries and come from a variety of backgrounds. While meeting with all of these interesting people, I began to notice a trend. The following are the most common themes that have emerged from my discussions with business owners:

√ Multiple streams of income can lead to more revenue streams and a better chance at success.

√ The process of starting a business is fun because it is challenging.

√ Capital is a primary consideration; make sure you have enough.

√ Friends and family weren't always supportive of the decision to start a business.

√ Problems were unavoidable along the way, but they found ways to deal with them.

√ Mentors, books, and online resources are essential planning tools.

√ Marketing doesn't have to cost a fortune.

√ The hours are long—usually 50 to 60 hours per week for several years.

√ Work/life balance must be made a priority.

√ It's difficult to imagine going back to working for someone else.

My Story: American Dreamin'

It was more than a decade ago when I got my first taste of the American dream. While most of my friends were still folding sweaters at the Gap, I was wearing a business suit and reporting to my first job in an office building that looked as big as Disneyland.

The monthly salary was handwritten on a Post-it note. I unfolded the golden slip and revealed a number that would not even cover my mortgage today—I was elated. I nodded my acceptance and reveled in the fact that my days of hourly wages were behind me.

My new prestigious career began in a customer service center where two dozen robotic agents answered an endless stream of incoming phone calls. The only window looked out into the lobby—or rather the lobby looked in on us. It was a room dubbed "The Fish Bowl," and our mere existence served as entertainment for all who entered the building.

The agents were graded on the volume of calls answered and customer satisfaction ratings. I took hundreds of calls each day, typing so fast that sometimes my knuckles cracked without warning. I took pride in my new role and delivered swift, perky service.

Several months later, it was time for a performance review. I anticipated kudos and instead received a cold reprimand from a drill sergeant disguised in designer clothes and flowery perfume. "Nobody could possibly take that many calls in a day," she said. "You must be doing something wrong."

Later that day, after raising my hand to request an unscheduled trip to the potty, I considered my predicament. This was corporate America! It was a real job and I was making a real monthly salary. I had benefits and paid vacation time and wore pumps to work. I was performing well yet somehow it wasn't good enough. I considered the alternatives and quickly realized that if I wanted to keep living the American dream, I had to suck it up.

My devotion to corporate America grew in direct proportion to the increases in salary and benefits. The next company I worked for presented me with stock options. I had no idea what they were, but they sounded fantastic! One of the best perks was in the break room: a refrigerator crammed full of bottles of Snapple. Stock options and free Snapple, I thought, this place is amazing.

The company was thriving and lavished us with logo-covered merchandise. I amassed a collection of coffee mugs, t-shirts, denim shirts, long sleeves, short sleeves, Frisbees, pens, paper clip dishes, CD holders, candy jars, jackets and even a fancy watch. The quarterly meetings were more like celebrations, complete with kegs of beer and platters of shrimp cocktail.

Eventually the flow of merchandise slowed to a halt. I wondered if there was some sort of delay in shipping and receiving. When the budget cuts were announced, I knew it was inevitable that the free Snapple would disappear too. I wondered how the entire office would handle the sugar crash as I watched the workers wheel out the prized refrigerator and replace it with a coin-operated soda machine.

Fast forward a few years to a new company, one that gave me stock options that split just a week after I started. By then I knew a thing or two about stocks, and this was a very good sign. They presented me with my own office, complete with a door and void of a window. I set up shop in my big white closet and fell in love with my new prestige and benefits package. It was a great time in the computer industry; the company was growing faster than the desks could be installed to accommodate all the new employees. I was in the heart of the Silicon Valley and it felt like winning the lottery.

The employee loyalty ran surprisingly deep. The logo-covered merchandise seemed bigger and better here. Some people even wore leather jackets with the company name emblazoned on the lapel. The break rooms were stocked with free bagels, sodas, and snacks and the company meetings were followed with live entertainment, beer, wine, and food. Twenty-five year old millionaires were born when the stock took off like a bottle rocket, and those of us who arrived on the scene just a little late watched them park their Porches with envy.

When the Dot Com Boom busted, the evening news was flooded with stories of corporate demise. I watched my friends lose their jobs faster than Donald Trump could say, "You're fired." Some companies didn't even have the decency to let their employees go with dignity. One news broadcast panned a rainy parking lot full of Silicon Valley workers who arrived to find a handwritten note on the locked front door of a large office building simply stating, "Out of Business."

I began to question the virtues of the corporate world. Sure, I still had a job. In fact, by then I had a house and a fancy car, thanks to those over-inflated stock options. I had a comfortable bank account, a hefty benefits package and a tidy 401K. But I was also working twelve hour days and just before my 30th birthday, I was diagnosed with an ulcer. That's when the fog rolled in.

There I was: a loyal worker who wore the company t-shirts to the gym and never took more bagels than I could actually eat. Though I was being rewarded financially for my efforts, I began to wonder how long it would last. How long would it be before another big layoff or corporate merger that sent hundreds of us to the unemployment line in our fancy cars? I considered the words of one boss who smirked like a child with too much power and said, "Everyone is replaceable." It was an epiphany. I was no different from anyone else. We were all as disposable as diapers.

I could go to another company, but for what? The impending doom lay in wait no matter where I went. No job was safe. Corporate America, it turns out, is full of high rollers who take out the little guys like they're shooting up characters in a video game. Nobody cares that these loyal workers have families to support and mortgages to pay. The massacre didn't even stop in December. Pink slips were handed out and people were sent home to enjoy the holidays without so much as a free turkey as a parting gift.

After more than a year of planning during my precious free time, I quit my job and opened Book Lovers Bookstore in Sacramento, CA. My relatives gasped in horror. "But you're giving up all that money and security," my father scolded. "No, Dad," I explained, "I'm finally putting my fate in my own hands." I thought entrepreneurship had an element of prestige, but most people looked at me like I had snakes in my hair.

True, entrepreneurship is risky. But so is driving on the highway at rush hour, falling in love or eating anything cooked in oil. The perception is that corporate America is the safety zone: that if you have a job there, you will be able to pay your mortgage and live the American dream. Sure the paychecks are cranked out twice each month from some mystical place called "Payroll," but that only matters if you're still *on* the payroll.

The big companies seem to let employees go whenever the quarterly numbers aren't up to par, yet corporate waste is infamous. As a small business owner, I would never blow money on beach balls with my company logo or regularly splurge on lavish parties to celebrate the fact that it is Friday. I watch my bottom line and do my best to show appreciation for the people who work for me.

Entrepreneurial life is good. My ulcer doesn't bother me anymore and my office has windows—lots of them. Do I miss corporate America? I did enjoy those free snacks, and for a while I missed the steady paycheck. But when they called and asked me to return, I knew that there weren't enough stock options on the NASDAQ to lure me back. Why would I do that? I have plenty of Snapple on hand and the only pink slip I ever have to worry about comes in the form of a phone message. Now that, my friends, is the American dream.

Organization Tips

Get a fresh spiral notebook and pen and keep them handy while you read this book. There are several exercises that suggest writing down your thoughts and ideas. Writing information down is also a great way to commit it to memory.

Create a system to gather articles and print outs from your business research so that you can easily locate them later. Start a binder or use file folders to manage your data. Here are some suggested titles for organizing your files:
√ General Business Information
√ Suppliers
√ Marketing Information
√ Industry Specific
√ Good Ideas

Apply this same organization concept to your Internet searches. Save websites to your "Favorites" folders so you can easily refer back to them. Use titles similar to those listed above.

For Internet Explorer users, here is how to create a file folder for your browser:

√ Open a browser window and select *Favorites* > *Organize Favorites*.

√ Click the *Create Folder* button

√ Type in a folder name (for example, *BUSINESS INFO*) and hit *<Enter>*.

√ Repeat until all folders are created.

To save a website to a Favorites folder, do the following:

√ Open the website in your browser.

√ Click on *Favorites* > *Add to Favorites*.

√ Select the appropriate folder and click *OK*.

To open websites stored in your Favorites folders:

√ Launch a browser window.

√ Click on *Favorites* then click on the appropriate folder and select the website to view.

Chapter 1

The Fear Factor

"Courage is resistance to fear, mastery of fear—not absence of fear."
—Mark Twain

A recent study revealed that 40% of American workers have considered starting a business and that fear is one of the main obstacles preventing them from moving forward. While it's not uncommon to have reservations about taking the leap into entrepreneurship, the good news is that there are a number of ways you can calm your nerves.

Starting a business can be a risky proposition, but some would argue that working in corporate America has its own element of risk. Many of us have been taught to believe in the steady paychecks and paid vacations offered by big corporations, but all you have to do is open up to the business page of your local newspaper to see reports of layoffs, corporate takeovers and restructuring.

The more than 19,000 unsuspecting employees of Enron were stunned by the news of the company's demise in 2001. More than 143 Internet companies disappeared completely in 2004, leaving employees scrambling to find work in a crowded job market. In the past 50 years, manufacturing jobs have gone from 34% of the workforce to a meager 14%.

When Oracle announced its acquisition of Pleasanton, California-based Peoplesoft, the doom was quickly cast in the headlines and across the small town that many Peoplesoft employees called home. On a gloomy Friday in January 2005, the employees of Peoplesoft—all of them—were instructed to pack up their offices and go home to await a Saturday UPS delivery that would contain either a termination notice or an offer letter. Not only did this have devastating effects for the more than 3000 people who lost their jobs, but the diminished morale of the remaining workers could linger for a long time.

In a time when job satisfaction has become an oxymoron and pink slips are being passed out in more creative and impersonal ways, many Americans are turning to entrepreneurship in search of a new sense of security. Yet for most people, deciding to start a business is not an easy decision.

Facing Down the Fear

If fear is holding you back from pursuing your dream of business ownership, remember that facing fears can make us triumphant and that we are forced to do it from the time we are born. Babies are plunged into a cold and foreign world and must learn to eat, crawl, walk and talk. If we let fear rule our lives, we would never learn to sleep with the lights off, go to school, drive, dance, sing, make a friend or fall in love. We would never evolve.

Can you remember a time in your life when you were afraid to do something? And how triumphant you felt once you faced the fear? If you've ever had to speak in front of an audience, attend a job interview, go to the dentist or learn a new skill, then you have already tackled many anxieties. Staring fear in the eyes may make your stomach queasy and your palms sweat, but it is exhilarating to move through it. Just ask anyone who has ever gone sky diving.

Keys to Reducing the Fear
of Business Ownership

It is perfectly normal to have some anxiety about starting a business, and I have yet to meet an entrepreneur who didn't experience some nerves starting out. But you can significantly reduce your anxiety level by utilizing these strategies:

Educate Yourself

Psychologists tell us that it is a lack of control that drives most fears. People who are afraid to fly are often treated for their phobias by seeing how a plane is operated. It can be difficult to give up control, especially for entrepreneurs. Most entrepreneurs are independent thinkers and leaders, so by nature we have a strong desire to oversee every aspect of our business.

Would you attempt to fly a plane without lessons? Of course not. But if you went through training and got your pilot's license, you would have the knowledge to achieve takeoff. The same is true when it comes to running a business. New business failure rates are high, in part because the owners fail to plan thoroughly. But you can't create a comprehensive plan if you don't know all that is involved.

When you educate yourself about starting and running a business, you gain control of your venture, automatically minimizing your fear factor. You have already learned many valuable life skills—you can read, write, balance your checkbook, take care of children, cook a meal, and perform your current job.

The fact is that we all have the ability to learn new skills and to expand our knowledge, which means that you have the tools necessary to learn how to run a business. If you need a reminder, just watch a child learning to ride a bike. He will fall off, probably several times, but with some effort and persistence, eventually he is able to soar on his own. It may take some work on your part, but once you begin to believe in your own abilities and master your fears, a wonderful new world will open up for you.

You have already begun your educational pursuit by reading this book so you are on the way to building a solid foundation. Here are some additional ways to learn about running a business:

√ Take classes through the U.S. Small Business Administration (www.sba.gov), through your local college or adult education center.

√ Join trade associations in your field to gain access to valuable resources and network with other members (more about locating trade associations in chapter five).

√ Subscribe to trade publications and business magazines.

√ Access free business startup resources on the Internet from sites like www.BusinessInfoGuide.com, www.IdeaCafe.com, and www.entrepreneur.com.

√ Network with other business owners even if they are in an entirely different industry. Every business owner has experiences, good and bad, and most will be happy to share their advice with you.

Build Your Confidence

Many would-be entrepreneurs lack the confidence to pursue their goals because they don't have faith in their own abilities. Everyone experiences moments of doubt, but if you tell yourself, "I can't do it" or "I'll never succeed," you risk creating a self-fulfilling prophecy. Eventually you start to believe all of the failure statements—and negative self talk will never move you ahead in life. If you don't believe in yourself, you can't expect anyone else to believe in you. Instead try telling yourself, "I can do this" or "I refuse to fail." Wouldn't you rather make this your self-fulfilling prophecy?

One of the best ways to build confidence is to arm yourself with the knowledge necessary to succeed. How confident would you feel if you had to take a test that you hadn't studied for? But if you studied for the test and took time to prepare, your confidence would increase and you would perform to your best ability. Now apply this concept to your business and watch your confidence grow.

You can also take an inventory of the areas of your life where you already shine. When do you feel at your best? Are you a great cook, gardener, parent, partner or friend? Do others envy you for your abilities in the office, at home or in sports? Are you a gifted artist, writer or teacher? We all have some talents and when you stop to think about yours, you will realize that your capabilities in other areas of your life can transfer into your business life.

It takes time to build confidence. While you work on it, try acting like you already have it. Some of the best business advice I ever received came from a sales manager who told me, "Just fake it. Walk into every room like you own the place." It turns out that if you exude confidence, others will be more likely to believe in you. Even if you have to fake it at first, not only will you boost the support of everyone in the room but eventually you will start to believe it yourself.

Get Some Experience

What if your doctor said that you needed an operation, and then added, "I haven't performed a surgery like this before, but I watched some in med school and I sort of remember how it's done." Would you climb up on the operating table?

If you want to open a restaurant but your only experience is dining in one, then you owe it to yourself and your future to learn what goes on behind the scenes. Consider getting a job or an internship in your area of interest. If you don't think you have time to do this, then you need to make the time. Carve out hours from your weekend, before or after work or even on your lunch hour. If you want it badly enough, you must find a way.

If you have some experience in your chosen field, it would still be wise to seek the advice of others who are already running a successful business in your industry. Business owners are typically eager to help others get started (as long as they don't view you as competition). Talk to business owners who aren't in your immediate geographic area. The best way to do this is to walk in and introduce yourself. You can also pick up the phone and offer to buy the owner lunch in exchange for some time to get your questions answered.

E-mail is a wonderful tool for communicating with entrepreneurs in your field. When I set out to open a bookstore, I surfed the Internet to locate bookstores all over the country. I wrote to dozens of store owners, told them I lived in Northern California (so they wouldn't be concerned about competition), and explained that I wanted to open a store. I listed several questions that I had about the business and thanked them profusely for their time. At least half of the business owners wrote back and each provided me with valuable advice. Now I often receive similar messages from people who find me and I always try to return the favor.

Break Down the Steps

It is overwhelming to start any kind of project that you have never faced before—just ask a bride who is planning her wedding for the first time. Many aspiring business owners don't know how to wade through all the requirements and details of starting a business. Even graduates with business degrees may not feel they have all the practical skills needed to start a company.

To make the planning process less overwhelming, break it down into small steps. Keep a running list of tasks that you need to complete with target dates. By setting target completion dates, you set a goal to work toward and keep yourself accountable for meeting each deadline. A business shouldn't be launched over a weekend; it is a process that takes time. Allow yourself enough time to complete your tasks thoroughly. You can start with the startup checklist provided in chapter five.

Consider the Worst Case Scenarios

Risk is unavoidable in business ownership. Even the most thoroughly-planned business could fail due to uncontrollable factors: economic recession, unexpected competition, natural disasters, illness and a litany of other scenarios. You may not want to think about everything that could go wrong, but the risk becomes even greater if you don't.

Many of us keep a roadside emergency kit in the trunks of our cars. We have jumper cables, a spare tire, flares and other supplies to aid in an emergency. Your business deserves the same preparation. Though you can't purchase a prepackaged business emergency kit at the gas station, you can create your own emergency plan by examining what could go wrong and how you will respond.

One of the primary considerations is your financial outlook. A gambler should never bet more than he is willing to lose, and the same is true for an entrepreneur. While there are stories of brave souls who have risked their life savings in pursuit of a dream and succeeded, there are just as many stories of failure. As you work through the exercises in this book and determine your financial foundation, consider how much you are willing to wager on your future.

While it can be unnerving to consider all of the factors that could go wrong, it can be liberating when you identify solutions to potential problems. No entrepreneur sets out to fail or struggle, but the reality is that you could face hard times and the more thought you give to this possibility early on, the more prepared you will be when you are facing difficult times.

Try This:

Think about all of the factors that are preventing you from moving forward and list them in a notebook. Once you have identified all of your fears and concerns, devote time to finding solutions for each. Putting your fears on paper allows you to face them head-on, and finding solutions will help you work through them. This should be an ongoing exercise. As new concerns arise, add them to your list and seek solutions.

Here are some examples:
√ I don't think I have enough money to quit my job and launch my business.

> *Possible Solution: I could start my business part-time while I keep my job. This would allow me time to learn about the business and decide whether or not it can be lucrative enough to earn a living. I don't have to quit my job to become an entrepreneur.*

√ What if the money runs out too soon?

> *Possible Solution: I could borrow from a friend or relative, bring in an investor, use my home equity line of credit or sell my weekend car. My uncle in Florida expressed interest in investing. I would like to do this on my own, but he would be available if I decide later that I need to add a partner.*

√ Who will run the business if I become ill or incapacitated?

Possible Solution: My father/brother/sister/daughter can run it until we find a suitable manager or until I return. I should also have a full staff after the first year so I may not have to worry about having extra help later on.

√ What if I launch the business and six months later decide I miss my job and that I made a big mistake?

Possible Solution: I could launch the business part-time before I quit my job and risk everything. Or I could get a job working in a similar business to make sure it's something I really want to do. I could also try to sell the business, bring in a partner or stick with it for two years until I have recouped my investment or until it is profitable and attractive to buyers.

√ I'm not sure I'm ready to run a business. I know I'm good at sales, but I'm not very good with paperwork and managing details.

Possible Solution: I could hire an accountant or employees that have strengths in areas where I have weaknesses. Or I could enlist a business partner with skills that complement mine.

√ I don't have time to plan and run a business. I have my job, my family and other commitments.

Possible Solution: I can dedicate at least an hour each day to working on my business plan. I can get up an hour earlier. I don't really need to watch the evening news and sitcoms every night. I could skip my book club meetings for awhile. I will make the time.

Entrepreneur Profile

Linda Formichelli
Freelance writer and author of *The Renegade Writer* and four
additional books
Blackstone, MA
www.twowriters.net and www.renegadewriter.com

Linda Formichelli plodded through a staggering 25 jobs before becoming a full-time freelance writer. She says, "I hated getting up at 6 a.m.; I hated fighting rush-hour traffic and I hated working my butt off to line the pockets of some rich executive."

When she relocated from California to Massachusetts with her husband so he could go to college, she took a gamble on her new career. "I saved up some money from my job at a small publishing company in Berkeley and I gave myself a few months to turn a profit. Luckily I managed to land several copywriting gigs as well as sell articles to small magazines and trade publications."

Overhead expenses are typically minimal for freelancers. With a husband in college and a limited budget, Formichelli set up her first office in the corner of her living room with a "Cheap Mac" and an imitation wood desk. She also maintained part-time status at her job and cut her hours back as she landed more writing assignments. Within months she was able to quit her side job completely and proclaim herself as fully self-employed. She says the strategy worked brilliantly. "My only regret is that I didn't do it sooner."

Most of Formichelli's skills are self-taught. She has never taken a journalism, business or writing class. She has a B.A. in Russian and an M.A. in Slavic Linguistics, which she calls, "Fun, but not very useful career-wise." To prepare for her home business, she read trade magazines and books about freelance writing. She also visited writer's web sites for support.

Of the 25 jobs that Formichelli held over the years, the one she kept the longest was the role of marketing assistant for a Dutch company that manufactures robotic vehicles. "I did a lot of business writing and that was very helpful when I started my writing career, as I did a lot of copywriting in my first few years. It also helped me learn how to keep organized, invoice clients, and market myself."

Freelance writing requires persistence. In order to find assignments, Formichelli solicited magazines with standard query letters (query letters are used by writers to propose article ideas to magazine editors). She had tremendous success with smaller publications, but wanted to work her way up to the bigger, better-paying publications.

"My career took off when I started breaking the rules I read about in writing magazines and books." The industry standard is to keep query letters short and sweet and no longer than a page. When an editor at Woman's Day said she preferred to see more meat in a query, Formichelli changed her strategy. "I started writing two and three page queries and immediately landed assignments from Woman's Day, Family Circle, and Redbook."

Defying industry standards worked so well for Formichelli that she co-authored a book outlining her controversial strategy with another freelance master, Diana Burrell. "The Renegade Writer: A Totally Unconventional Guide to Freelance Writing Success" advises writers on ways to negotiate better contracts, avoid using formulaic pitches in query letters and to pick up the phone and call an editor if a query has gone ignored.

Successful book sales and notoriety have generated even more demand for Formichelli's talents. She has written for over 120 magazines to date, including such prestigious titles as Parenting Magazine, Family Circle, USA Weekend, Men's Health, Cooking Light, and Psychology Today. She also offers an online course on how to write for magazines (visit: www.twowriters.net/ lessonindex.html *for details).*

She gave up copywriting long ago and says that now she works an average of 20 hours per week. "When I started out, I worked day and night, seven days per week. But I've learned how to write fast so I can get more work done in less time. I'm also writing for better-paying clients, so I can write less and still make the same amount of money."

On a typical work day, Formichelli reports that she gets up between 7:00 and 9:00 a.m. and begins by checking e-mail. She tries to schedule phone interviews for the morning so she gets them out of the way. Even with all her experience, she says she still finds interviews intimidating.

If she has an article to write, she either stretches out on the couch in her living room or treks down to the local bookstore. Other daily tasks involve brainstorming new story ideas, writing and following up on query letters, chasing down late payments, and crafting thank you notes to interviewees.

Freelance writing carries the stigma of being a lonely profession. When Formichelli first moved to the East Coast, she didn't know anyone and worked long hours while establishing herself in the industry. Eventually she found a network of local writers that she met online and made friends through her neighborhood karate center. "My job is a job and I try not to let it take over my life. When I'm on my deathbed, I won't wish I had worked

more, but I'll definitely regret if I had let work get in the way of
friendship."

Formichelli's husband, W. Eric Martin, is also a successful
freelance writer and they occasionally help each other with
assignments. Her family has also been a source of encouragement.
"My parents were so proud to see my name in magazines! Many
people's friends tell them they're crazy to become a writer, but
that wasn't the case for me. I had a lot of support."

Successful freelancers, like all business owners, know that
marketing is crucial. "Many writers hate marketing because it
goes against the starving artist image they have in their minds,"
says Formichelli. "But I love marketing my articles and books
– even more than I like writing them." She also likes to give
presentations on writing advice at bookstores and conferences
and remains active on Internet message boards for writers.

As for her plans for the future, she says, "I really haven't given
it any thought. I guess I'm just happy with the way things are
right now."

Q&A with Linda Formichelli:

What advice would you give to aspiring freelancers?

"Don't be afraid of rejection – and believe me, you'll get a
lot of it. Only 38 percent of my ideas have been accepted for
publication, which means 62 percent of my ideas were rejected
– and most of them were rejected by several magazines. If I had
let that bother me, I would have never made it as a freelance
writer. You have to have a thick skin in this business.

Also, trade magazines are a great market for aspiring writers.
Many people overlook them because they're not glamorous and

they tend not to pay as much as consumer magazines, but they're often desperate for good writers and very easy to work with."

Are there books, websites or other resources you would recommend?

*"I like 'Dojo Wisdom for Writers' by Jennifer Lawler and 'Ready...Aim...Specialize!' by Kelly James-Enger. Every writer should also have the latest version of 'Writer's Market', which is a directory of magazines that accept freelance submissions. Once you have a little experience, I'd suggest subscribing to Freelance Success (*www.freelancesuccess.com*), which costs $90 per year."*

What would you do differently if you could start all over?

"I would have done it sooner!"

Any final words of wisdom?

"One mistake that just about every aspiring magazine writer makes is to write an article and then look for a home for it. Editors usually want to see queries – not an entire manuscript. That way, when they give you the assignment they can specify word count, slant, who you should interview, etc. So if you have an idea, write the query first (Jenna Glatzer's book has advice on how to write a good query) – then, if you get the assignment, you can write the article."

Chapter 2

Is Entrepreneurship for Me?

"Dreams that come true can be as unsettling as those that don't."
–Brett Butler, 'Knee Deep in Paradise'

According to the U.S. Small Business Administration, small businesses (defined as companies with 500 or fewer employees):

√ Represent 99.7 percent of all employers.
√ Pay 44.3 percent of total U.S. private payroll.
√ Generated 60 to 80 percent of net new jobs annually over the last decade.
√ Create more than 50 percent of non-farm private gross domestic product (GDP).
√ Are employers of 39 percent of high tech workers (such as scientists, engineers, and computer workers).
√ Are 53 percent home-based and 3 percent franchises.
√ Made up 97 percent of all identified exporters and produced 29 percent of the known export value in fiscal year 2001.

In the United States, there is one female entrepreneur for every 1.5 male entrepreneurs. Of minority-owned businesses, 39.5 percent were Hispanic-owned, 30 percent Asian-owned, 27.1 percent Black-owned, and 6.5 percent American Indian-owned.

Around 50 percent of U.S. entrepreneurial activity is accounted for by individuals between 24 and 44 (compared to 55 percent worldwide). Americans between 45 and 64 years of age account for 36 percent of the U.S. entrepreneurial activity, much higher than the global average of 22 percent.

The Survival Rate of New Businesses

The number of businesses estimated to open and close each year averages roughly 10 percent of the total number of small businesses in the U.S. In 2003, the estimates reveal that 572,900 new firms entered the marketplace and 584,800 businesses closed.

Two-thirds of new employer firms survive at least two years, and about half survive at least four years. Owners of about one-third of the firms that closed said their firm was successful at closure. Major factors in a firm remaining open include an ample supply of capital, the fact that a firm is large enough to have employees, the owner's education level, and the owner's reason for starting the firm in the first place, such as freedom for family life or wanting to be one's own boss.

Business survival also varies by industry and demographics. The industry with the highest 1992–1996 survival rate for firms owned by white non-Hispanics was oil and gas extraction (82 percent survival rate over the four-year period). African Americans were most successful in legal services (79 percent), and Hispanic and Asian Americans in health services (66 percent and 76 percent, respectively).

To read more about these business statistics, visit: www.sba.gov/advo/stats/sbfaq.html. While there you may also want to read *Business Success: Factors Leading to Surviving and Closing Successfully* by Brian Headd, Center for Economic Studies, U.S. Bureau of the Census, Working Paper #CES-WP-01-01, January 2001; Advocacy-funded research by Richard J. Boden (Research Summary #204).

Why Do Businesses Fail?

According to statistics cited on the U.S. Small Business Administration website, 50% of businesses fail within the first year and as many as 95% fail within the first five years. These statistics are startling, but keep in mind that many business licenses are applied for on a whim and then the owner later decides not to pursue a business. It is likely that these occurrences affect the statistics. The fact remains that an alarming number of new businesses fail each year. The SBA lists the following as the most common reasons for failure:

√ Lack of experience
√ Insufficient capital (money)
√ Poor location
√ Poor inventory management
√ Over-investment in fixed assets
√ Poor credit arrangements
√ Personal use of business funds
√ Unexpected growth
√ Competition
√ Low sales

In examining these factors, the common denominator seems to be a lack of planning. If you are willing to put forth the effort to meticulously plan your endeavor, you will have a significant advantage over the businesses that aren't managed properly. Keep the above factors in mind and address them long before you flip on the open sign.

Is Corporate America Really Providing Security?

The new millennium has marked a time in America when unemployment rates have reached staggering levels. Many of us have watched the pink slips handed out to our friends and loved ones or have been victims of this cruel fate ourselves.

Who can forget the financial disasters experienced by the employees of Enron? Not only did they lose their jobs, but many had the bulk of their retirement savings invested in a company they believed in. It was an example of employee loyalty that ultimately led to hundreds of cases of financial devastation.

Perhaps we have been conditioned to believe in the sanctity of corporate America. Our parents' generation went to work for a company and stayed there for 35 years, retired and collected a pension. Many of us learned to follow in these same footsteps.

But times have changed and today there are few companies that even offer pension plans. Even fewer are the numbers of people who stay put in the same company for 30+ years. Instead, many Americans devote several years to a company, then move on to a different company seeking better salaries, working conditions or status. Just as it's easy for employees to move from job to job, the corporations themselves often treat employees as expendable resources.

This economy and the massive job losses have prompted a renewed interest in business ownership. If corporate America isn't safe, then what are the alternatives? Many believe the only option is to put their fate in their own hands.

Do You Have What it Takes to Be an Entrepreneur?

Are you self-motivated? Do your trust yourself with the responsibility? Will you be up at all hours questioning your decision to leave your job behind? To become a business owner, you must be willing to take risks. Can you live with the choices you make? Will you be devastated if your business fails—and do you have faith in your ability to recover? With a new business failure rate rivaling the divorce rate in the U.S., there are no guarantees that even the greatest idea will make it.

Owning a business means giving up the benefits provided by big companies. You will no longer have paid vacations or sick days. Medical and dental benefits are extraordinarily expensive in the U.S. Can you obtain coverage through your spouse's company? You won't have a 401K or pension plan and will need to locate one on your own.

Entrepreneurs I polled suggested that it takes the following traits to be a successful business owner:
√ A willingness to do what it takes to get the job done.
√ Belief in yourself and your business. You can't sell something you don't believe in.
√ Tenacity, perseverance and drive are all integral to your success.
√ Self motivation is critical. Your business will fail faster than an Olympic sprint if you let too many things slide or sleep in until noon every day.

The Pros and Cons of Owning Your Own Business

Pros:
√ You're the boss. You set your own hours and make (or break) all the rules.
√ Your destiny and your earnings potential are in your own hands.
√ There is a sense of accomplishment when you own your own business.
√ You can upgrade to an Executive membership at Costco and shop an hour earlier than the rest of the neighborhood. My local warehouse store serves bagels and coffee to the business members!
√ Your business card can have any title you want to use; President, CEO, Owner, Founder, etc. The title on my bookstore card is "Chief Book Officer."

√ You decide on the dress code. Many people who work at home admit to working in pajamas or sweats.

√ You hold the power to make your business as large as you want it to be.

Cons:

√ Loss of benefits. You will have to pay for your own medical and dental insurance, which is unfortunately quite costly in the U.S.

√ No more paid vacations or sick days.

√ All legal and financial responsibility falls on your shoulders (though some risks can be minimized by incorporating your business).

√ Long hours. Most new business owners work 50 to 60 hours per week or more. While many people start their own businesses with the ultimate goal of having a more flexible schedule and lifestyle, it can take years to get your business to that point.

√ Employee management. You will be responsible for hiring, firing, payroll, benefits, and filling in when employees are out.

√ Credit will be difficult to rebuild. Without a steady income, it will likely take at least two years to reestablish your credit worthiness. It is not impossible to get a loan as a new business owner, but it's certainly more difficult and you may end up paying higher interest rates as a result.

Can You Afford the Time?

The financial investment is an obvious consideration that we will discuss later on, but what about the precious commodity of time? While your ultimate goal in starting your own business may be to have more time to spend with your family, it may take years before that becomes a reality. Most business owners work very long hours, especially in the early years.

Do you have room in your life for a business? Will your family understand and accommodate your new schedule? If you are already committed to a full schedule of activities such as coaching your child's soccer team, running the Girl Scout meetings, babysitting other people's children, caring for an aging parent, managing very small children or going to school yourself, you will need to decide if you are willing to sacrifice some of your other commitments. In order to make your business a success, you need to devote as much attention to it as possible—particularly in the early stages.

Making the Decision

If you are still unsure if entrepreneurship is right for you, don't give up yet. You can still proceed with planning your business and let your research guide you. You may start a business plan and decide that you have chosen the wrong course, and then have to start again. Learn to listen to your gut instincts, and follow your heart. Sometimes when we are very quiet, we can suddenly discover exactly what it is that we should be doing.

Try This:

Make your own Pros and Cons list and ask yourself these questions:
√ What are the benefits that you see for launching your business?
√ Are they realistic?
√ What are the negative aspects of your venture?
√ Can you live with the cons list?
√ Am I self-motivated?
√ Do I trust myself with the responsibility?
√ Will I worry excessively about my decision to leave my job behind?
√ Will I be devastated if my business fails?
√ Will I be mentally and financially able to recover?

Entrepreneur Profile

Lynn Colwell
Bloom 'n Grow Coaching for Life
Post Falls, ID
www.bloomngrow.net

Lynn Colwell has been a corporate communications specialist, a public relations director, freelance writer, photographer, childbirth educator, and children's clothing designer. But after being laid off, she decided it was time for a career change. She embarked on a graduate degree in counseling and after a year, decided it wasn't the right choice for her. Instead, she shifted gears and sought training to become a personal coach.

"I knew it would take some time to get myself up to speed as a coach, but I had no fears about being a poor coach. I felt pretty confident based on my past experience," says Colwell. The 59 year-old mother of three and grandmother of four says that her family and friends provided great support with her new business decision. "When I told them about coaching, every single one of them gave me a thumbs-up. They all could see it was a perfect fit."

Colwell didn't write a business plan and makes no apologies for her decision. "In my experience, most successful entrepreneurs are simply not focused people. We're dreamers, inventors, incautious, outside-the-box thinkers." She also says that her excitement for her new business kept her up at night, a sure sign that she was onto something great.

The financing for the business came from her own savings. She cautions that it may not seem like an expensive business to launch, but there are many costs involved. "The training is not cheap," says Colwell. She points out the need for a good long distance plan, an 800 number, high speed Internet connection, website development and maintenance, design of logos, membership dues, and books.

To market the business, Colwell works hard to get the word out. Her best strategy is offering free half-hour coaching calls to people all over the world. Personal coaching is an up-and-coming service and Colwell is often tasked with educating potential clients about the benefits. "I explain that coaching is like sex. I can tell you all about it, but until you try it yourself, you really have no idea how great it can be." This usually provokes a laugh and leads to scheduling the free call.

Her website acts as another important marketing tool. "If I can get people to the website where they can meet me and explore what coaching is, they often will want the complimentary call." Colwell also peruses a lot of message boards and offers free advice while using her signature to advertise her complimentary service.

The issues people bring to Colwell range from building a business to building a life. She says she challenges her clients to take action by experimenting with ideas or trying new behaviors. "My coaching business is built on my desire to help other people, but I am not a therapist and do not attempt to be one. I am very clear about what I will and will not provide my clients."

Her self-designed website is packed with details about her offerings and includes articles she has written, recommendations for services she likes and an offer to subscribe to her free newsletter. The warm and friendly site invites clients to experience the help that Colwell provides.

A typical work week ranges between 30 to 50 working hours and Colwell adheres to a regimented schedule. She arrives at her computer by 7:30 each morning and talks with four to six clients each day. She schedules her free calls on Mondays and Fridays and her regular client calls mid-week.

Since working from home can be isolating, she tries to schedule lunch dates on Mondays and Fridays. "I spend at least half the day e-mailing and contributing to various websites. I also write articles, maintain my website, and look for opportunities to develop my business."

Colwell says when she's not with a client, she takes a five minute break each hour and exercises, cleans up or does anything that gets her moving. "In addition, most days at 10 a.m. and 3:30 p.m., I walk outside or on the treadmill for half an hour."

Some unhappy coaches have expressed their dismay over Colwell's pricing. "The biggest challenge I've faced had to do with pricing my service. Most coaches charge high fees. I was not comfortable doing that for many reasons. I believe so strongly in coaching that I want it to be available to as many people as possible, so I decided to become the 'Wal-Mart' of coaches, offering value at a low price."

Colwell has a few favorite books that she recommends to aspiring entrepreneurs: "Feel the Fear and Do it Anyway" by Susan Jeffers; "What Should I Do With My Life?" By Po Bronson; "A Complaint is a Gift" by Janelle Barlow and Claus Moller; "Hey I'm the Customer" by Ron Willingham; and "Positively Outrageous Service" by T. Scott Gross.

As for advice for entrepreneurs, Colwell says, "Have a dream but be a realist. Don't expect someone else to make your dream a reality. You'll have to work hard, do things you neither want to do nor are particularly good at. Look to others who have gone before you. Read, ask questions, make friends, and don't be afraid to ask for help."

She cautions that being an entrepreneur is not for everyone and just because you don't like working for someone else doesn't mean you'll like working for yourself any better. "But if you aren't responsible for the well-being of anyone other than yourself, why not give it a try? You may just be successful beyond your wildest dreams and if you're not, the world will go on turning and you will have had a fascinating experience."

Quick Tip:

Create an idea journal. Use a medium-sized spiral notebook to keep track of all your business and marketing ideas. This is a great way to make sure you don't forget them later.

Chapter 3

What Kind of Business Should I Start?

"Creativity comes from trust. Trust your instincts."
–Rita Mae Brown

It's not uncommon to reach your 30s, 40s or even 50s and still wonder, "What do I want to be when I grow up?" Not everyone is born with a desire to pursue a specific career, and sometimes those that do know what they want end up changing their minds. But when it comes to running a business, you can increase your chances of success by pursuing something you can be passionate about.

Lifestyle Requirements

Whatever business you choose has to meet the needs of your lifestyle requirements. To define what those are, consider how you live today. Do you eat dinners out often? Enjoy shopping for items that aren't necessarily essential? Do you stop for a gourmet coffee every morning? Are there areas where you are willing to cut back?

Many new business owners make sacrifices, like moving to a less expensive home to reduce the overall cost of living. Are you willing to make these compromises in order to bring your dream to fruition? Decide on what you absolutely must live with and what you can do without. You may be able to live well below your means if in exchange, you are able to pursue your passions and do something that you love. Few businesses are wildly successful right out the gate, though over time and with hard work, your position could change for the better.

You're a Winner!

Let's say you've just won a lottery for $500,000—congratulations! It's not enough to retire on, but it's enough to make some decisions about your future. Think about what you would do if you won a large chunk of money. Of course it's fun to imagine paying off your debts and sharing your good fortune with the people you love, but what would you do with the rest of the money? What kind of business would you start if money was no object?

Try This:

Write your answers to the following questions in your note-book:
√ What does your ideal work life look like? Do you want to travel? Work early in the day and have your afternoons free? Work from home? Work from an office? Do you like working 50 hour weeks?
√ What kind of business would you start if you had endless resources?

Evaluate Your Interests, Talents, and Skills

What do you like and dislike about your current job and jobs you've had in the past? Do you love writing business documents? Do you hate calculating numbers? By identifying your likes and dislikes, you can see with more clarity where some of your interests lie and which tasks you want to avoid. If you hate sitting in an office all day, then starting a business that will shackle you to a desk is probably not the best option. But also consider whether you hate being indoors all day, or whether you simply don't like the place you are currently working.

Try This:

Make a list of your interests, talents, skills, likes, and dislikes. Prioritize the items in the "Likes" column that are most important to you. If spending time with your family is a top priority, then opening a restaurant might not be a good choice due to the long hours required. Instead, you might consider selling a food product to stores or opening a catering business.

The trick is to brainstorm business ideas and find one that you will be passionate about, one that will meet your desired standard of living and your quality of life criteria. Someone who doesn't like being chained to a desk should not choose a business that requires her to be stuck in an office all day. The good news is that as an entrepreneur, you get to make these decisions for yourself. Perhaps you are good with numbers and you're thinking about becoming a mortgage broker, but you don't want to be stuck in an office all day. If you are serving clients in your area, won't you also be required to meet with them? Could you find a way to meet with them at their place of business or over lunch?

This list should also help you identify your weaknesses. If you hate to write, then you probably shouldn't start a local newspaper (although if you have the right budget, you can hire writers and focus on other aspects of the business). If crunching numbers makes your brain hurt, then you won't find joy in running a bookkeeping business. For that matter, you will probably dread keeping your own books and should build a bookkeeping service into your business budget.

Spend some time with this exercise and look for a theme in your lists. If you identify a business that interests you, but it doesn't meet your lifestyle requirements, then expand on the idea and see if there is a different type of business in that field that would better suit you.

Could Your Talent or Hobby Net You Some Profits?

Whether you are a musician, an artist, a writer, a crafter, an athlete, an entertainer or a chef, you may be able to find a business that takes advantage of these talents. Gifted writers can make money selling freelance articles or offering copywriting services to businesses. Antique collectors can open a shop or sell their wares on eBay. Artists can sell original pieces or use their creative talents to produce items for resale like greeting cards with unique images or t-shirts. The choices are abundant, especially when it's something you are truly passionate about.

Interview Family and Friends

By asking the people closest to you for input, you may gain some surprising insight. Perhaps your best friend will remind you of your culinary talents or your grandmother will admire your decorating skills. Maybe your brother will tell you that he always thought you would end up working with animals because you rescued all the neighborhood strays. If for nothing else, asking those closest to you will breed discussion about your future and may lead to the spark of inspiration you are seeking.

Try This:

Contact the following people and ask them to answer the question, "What do you imagine me doing for a living?"
√ Spouse/Significant Other
√ Mom
√ Dad
√ Sibling #1
√ Sibling #2
√ Grandparent
√ Aunt or Uncle
√ Best Friend
√ Friend #2
√ Friend #3

Did You Have a Childhood Dream that Got Squelched Along the Way?

Did you previously yearn to work with children or want to be a detective like Columbo? What interests did you have in your childhood? Ask your parents what you talked about being when you grew up. Were you a talented performer who left the joy behind to earn a heftier paycheck? Years of working for "the man" can erode your sense of self so try reflecting back in time.

Start Looking at the Business World Through a New Set of Eyes

Every business you see was started somewhere by someone. The dry cleaner you visit weekly, the grocery store where you shop, the quaint coffee shop on the corner, and your favorite take-out restaurant were all born from somebody's dream. Pay attention to every business you encounter. Is the owner present? If so, does he or she look happy? Tired? Frantic? What are the pros and cons of running each kind of business?

A retail business is typically a 6 or 7 day per week effort. Restaurants require long hours, food spoilage management, health department inspections and a lot of staff. Service businesses, like coaches, writing, and design, are often started by an owner who provides the service himself. He may be able to use sub-contractors for some of the work as the business grows.

Talk to business owners wherever you go. Ask them about the pros and cons of what they do. Who better to advise you on your future than those who are actually living some version of it?

Go to the Bookstore or the Library

I personally believe that books give you the best opportunity to self-educate. You can learn about virtually any topic under the sun just by reading a book. Spend some time in the business section and read some of the books suggested in this book. You never know where you will find inspiration.

Learn About the Industry

If you have a general interest, you can use the Internet to learn more about an industry and perhaps find some inspiration or a business idea. Search the Internet for topics of interest such as sports, writing or public services.

√ Business Info Guide offers free links to many industry-specific resources including antiques & collectibles, sports, health & fitness, retail, food-related businesses, Internet businesses and more: www.BusinessInfoGuide.com.

√ Competia offers links to industry information: www.competia. com/express/index.html

√ Visit business message boards for ideas. One great forum is hosted by www.IdeaCafe.com.

√ Another good forum to visit is www.Business-Idea.com.

When You Still Don't Know What to Do...

So you've considered the suggestions thus far and you still have no idea what to do next. Don't give up! Keep at it. Carve some time out every day to focus on your life plan. Get up an hour earlier in the morning, use your lunch hour or stay up an hour late, but whatever you do, devote some time to mapping out your future.

Keep doing the exercises listed here. Spend time reading business message boards, websites and magazines. Jot down topics that interest you and learn more about them. The process may take some time, but the end result should be well worth it.

In my case, I knew I wanted to be a writer but I wasn't sure what to do with my dream. I had been fretting about my future. I wanted to escape the high tech industry and desperately wanted to take control of my destiny.

My epiphany happened when I least expected it. One Friday night, as I lay on the couch in my usual exhausted state from another long week in corporate America, the movie *You've Got Mail* came on TV. As I watched listlessly, I noticed Meg Ryan's character running her children's bookstore. I literally sprang to my feet. "A bookstore!" It was like I had known it all along and it suddenly made sense.

Though owning a bookstore wasn't my primary dream, I have been a book-aholic for as long as I can remember. My strategy would be to start a business that I could be passionate about and eventually run part-time with the help of employees. Once I turned it into "passive income" (income you generate when you're not working), I would have time to focus on my writing goals. It was a perfect solution and with much hard work, one that has worked out well for me.

I began researching the idea that very night and never looked back. So if you get discouraged, don't give up. You just never know where inspiration will strike.

Ten Easy Businesses to Start Part-Time or Full-Time:

1. **Freelance Writer** – Freelance writers write articles for newspapers and magazines or copy for businesses. Most articles require research and must be well-written and suited to the style of the publication. Publications typically pay $.10 to $2.00 per word. Businesses also contract writers to create reports, press releases, advertising copy, and other special projects.

2. **Virtual Assistant** – A Virtual Assistant (VA) provides administrative services to small businesses that don't have a staff to handle these duties. VAs can perform a variety of tasks for clients including contact database management, writing and sending business letters, designing brochures, and creating newsletters. VAs should advertise their services to Realtors and small business owners and can charge by the hour or by project.

3. **Computer Tutor** – Computer tutors teach students how to navigate the Internet, access e-mail, set up a new computer, and use programs like Word, Excel, Powerpoint, and QuickBooks. These services can be delivered one-on-one or in classes held at local adult learning campuses, retirement centers, and churches. Tutors can charge by the hour or a flat fee for class registration.

4. **Pet Sitter** – Pet sitters provide in-home pet care while pet owners are on vacation. Services offered typically include feeding and playing with the animals, yard or litter box cleanup, dog walking, plant watering, newspaper and mail gathering, and rotating lights. Pet sitters usually charge a fee per visit and charge extra to care for additional pets.

5. **Landscaper** – Landscaping services can range from lawn mowing, hedge trimming and weed maintenance to sprinkler installation and designing complete landscapes for homes and businesses. Landscapers usually charge by the job and offer weekly or bi-weekly maintenance services to clients.

6. **EBay Trading Assistant** – Trading assistants provide a service to members of their community by acting as sales brokers on eBay. Trading assistants contract with clients to list items for sale, collect fees from buyers, ship the items and then take a percentage of the profits—usually between 30 to 50%. This is an excellent service to offer people who are not computer

savvy, yet have items they would like to sell online. EBay offers a directory where trading assistants can be listed for free.

7. **Homemade Crafter** – Crafters who create quality goods such as knitted items, wooden wares, ornaments, clothing, home décor, and even baked goods can sell their products for a profit. Crafts can be sold at flea markets, street fairs, trade shows, in-home parties, community events, or through a website.

8. **Notary Service Provider** – Notary service providers witness the signing of important documents such as real estate transactions, insurance, marriage and divorce papers, and letters. A state exam is required for certification. This service is in high demand with Realtors and title companies and can be conducted from home, in restaurants or title company offices. Fees are usually charged as a flat rate per service.

9. **Resume Designer** – Resume designers help job seekers by crafting professional resumes and cover letters. Resumes can be created using special software or with templates and a word processing program. This service is in demand with college students and all kinds of job seekers. Fees range from $50 to $250 depending on the level of work involved.

10. **Cleaning Service Provider** – Cleaning service providers typically target homes and businesses. Service offerings include cleaning of windows, floors, bathrooms, kitchens, work areas, and offices. General cleaning supplies are usually needed and services can be billed by the hour or on a contract basis.

Buying an Existing Business

Businesses are sold for all kinds of reasons: they aren't profitable, the owners are ill, relocating, retiring, or pursuing other interests.

When considering buying an established business, make sure to get professional assistance. An accountant, business consulting company or business broker can help you with the details, and you will also need the consult of a lawyer.

In some cases, it can be slightly easier to obtain a loan when buying an existing business versus starting a new business. Banks like businesses that are established and have a successful track record. It could also help if you have experience in a related field or industry, adding to your credibility as a good credit risk.

When evaluating a business, you will want to see at least the previous two years of bookkeeping records and review them thoroughly. Ask questions about any discrepancies or concerns. The owner should also provide you with tax returns for the prior three years, a list of assets that will be transferred with the purchase along with the assets that won't be transferred, and lease information.

You have the right to ask lots of questions and expect thorough answers. Here are some questions you should ask:
√ How long have you been in business?
√ Did you start the business or buy/acquire it from someone else?
√ Have you always been in this location?
√ Why are you selling the business?
√ Are there any outstanding debts that would be transferred with the business?
√ Do you have a written manual of operating procedures that you can share with me?
√ Are there special licensing or insurance requirements for this business?
√ How many employees do you have and how many hours do they work each week?

√ How do you manage inventory?
√ Do you use any special software or programs that I should know about?
√ What kind of training can you provide? (Many sellers offer at least two weeks, but sometimes longer depending on the business.)
√ Are you available for consultation after the purchase is complete?

The owner may also offer to carry some of the financing. This can not only help you afford to buy the business, but can act as added assurance that the business is viable and successful. No seller should want to carry papers on a business that is doomed for failure. There are also ways to set up an agreement to protect the new owner from any claims against the prior ownership.

Beware of business opportunity scams. These are far too common across the Internet and in the classified section of the newspaper. Remember the old saying, if it sounds too good to be true, it probably is. Trust your instincts and proceed with caution.

Your instincts are also important when meeting with a seller. If you suspect that you aren't getting complete information, or your questions aren't being answered thoroughly, don't ignore your feelings. Press for answers and if you don't get them, it is probably best to move on to a different opportunity.

No matter what the situation, make sure to seek your own representation when negotiating the purchase of a business. You will need the services of an accountant and a lawyer and may want to enlist a business broker. To locate professionals in your community, ask your business contacts or your local chamber of commerce. There should also be listings in the yellow pages.

Additional Resources:

√ Information from the *Wall Street Journal* Small Business site: www.bizbuysell.com/cgi-bin/xhome?J=J

√ *Entrepreneur* magazine lists business opportunities at: www. entrepreneur.com/bizoppzone/0,4997,,00.html

√ The SBA offers advice for buyers: www.sba.gov/starting_ business/startup/buy.html

√ Books: *"How to Buy a Business"* by Richard A. Joseph, and *"Buying Your Own Business: Identifying Opportunities, Analyzing True Value, Negotiating the Best Terms, Closing the Deal" (Expert Advice for Small Businesses)* by Russell Robb.

Buying a Franchise

This is another scenario that warrants the hiring of some professional assistance. There are numerous pros and cons to owning franchises. While you receive brand recognition and established operating procedures, you also have to follow many rules and send a portion of your profits back to corporate headquarters every month. Some franchises don't generate enough profits to sustain the owner and work best when you own more than one location.

As with buying any business, make sure you ask a lot of questions. To get a better idea, you may want to interview several franchise operations so you can compare their offerings. Each should be willing to send you a packet of information. Here are some questions to use in your investigation process:

√ How many franchise operations do you have?

√ Where are they located?

√ What is the initial franchise fee?

√ What is the royalty fee? (Franchises generally charge royalties equal to three to six percent of revenues per location, though some fee rates are higher and some require a flat fee on an ongoing basis.)

√ How much money can I expect to make each year?

√ What services do you provide? Help with licensing, design, layout, inventory, etc.? (Make sure to get commitments in writing.)

Investigate your options carefully. Ask for references and call every one of them. A friend of mine, we'll call him Joe, investigated a food-service franchise a few years ago. Joe asked for references and called each one. The very first person he called was surprisingly negative. The reference told Joe that the hours were long and that he could only expect to make about $40,000 per year—if he was lucky. He also rattled off some gripes about the corporate office. Though the franchise listed this person as a positive reference, Joe was able to get his specific questions answered honestly. The time he took to make the calls prevented him from pursuing a business that didn't fit his lifestyle requirements.

One franchise owner I interviewed is very happy with his decision. He owns three food-service locations that practically run themselves. He works an average of twenty hours per week and was able to take the entire summer off to spend with his family. But he does admit that getting the businesses started and operating smoothly took a lot of time and effort.

Yet another franchise owner, Steve Rumberg, is very happy with his decision to invest in a real estate franchise location. You can read his profile at the end of chapter five.

As with any business, there are pros and cons to consider. Be sure to do your homework so you can make an educated decision.

Additional Resources:

√ *Franchise Times* magazine: www.franchisetimes.com/

√ *Entrepreneur* magazine: www.entrepreneur.com/ franzone/0,4670,,00.html

√ Resources from the SBA: www.sba.gov/starting_business/ startup/franchise.html, www.franchiseregistry.com/

√ The Federal Trade Commission regulates franchise fraud information and provides guidelines for franchisees: www. ftc.gov/bcp/franchise/netfran.htm

√ Locate franchise trade shows through Franchise Handbook. com: www.franchise1.com/shows/

√ Books: *"Tips and Traps When Buying a Franchise"* by Mary E. Tomzack, and *"Franchise Bible"* by Erwin J. Keup

Entrepreneur Profile

Barry Schmell and Joseph Costa
De La Sole Footwear San Francisco, CA
www.delasole.com

San Francisco's famous Castro District is brimming with shops and restaurants, art galleries, coffee shops, and people. But partners in business and in life, Barry Schmell and Joe Costa, noticed something was missing: a shoe store. So they set out to change a little part of their favorite neighborhood.

With over 15 years of retail experience, Costa had longed to start his own business for years. Schmell, a long-time veteran of the Silicon Valley, says, "I did not always want to go into business for myself, but between the volatility of the high-tech industry and the strong desire of my business partner to start a business, I decided to do it."

Like most entrepreneurs, Costa and Schmell experienced some nerves about starting their venture. "Our biggest fear was not knowing what we needed to know. We lacked confidence since neither of us had started a new business, yet we both knew we could run and manage an existing business," says Costa.

To combat the fear factor, the pair enrolled in a business startup course through San Francisco's Renaissance Center. The intensive class lasted several months and when it was over, the duo had a solid business plan and a new level of confidence. They also read numerous business books and interviewed other business owners to learn from their experiences.

They relied on the Internet for much of their market research but decided they also needed some industry experience. "We attended the World Shoe Association conference in Las Vegas before we started the business," says Costa. "It helped us learn the shoe industry by meeting with vendors and selecting product lines."

To finance the business, they used a home equity loan. "This is the best route since it offers the financial independence and best industry rates. The downside is the personal liability, but that is true no matter how you finance the business," says Schmell.

The high price of real estate in San Francisco meant that they would have to make the most of a small retail space. They embarked on renovations that caused some frustrations along the way. "During construction we trusted our landlord and designer more than we should have. Next time, we'll get more in writing." Though the renovations delayed the store opening by several weeks, De La Sole celebrated its "Grand Unlacing" in February of 2004, an event that was also attended by then San Francisco Mayor Willie Brown.

Though the new business owners received a lot of support from their network of business contacts, not everyone was enthusiastic about their shoe store ambitions. "My family thought I was crazy since I had come from the high-paying software industry. Little did they know how volatile that industry has become," says Schmell. "Our friends were very supportive because they knew what we wanted to accomplish."

Costa runs the store full-time, averaging 50 hours per week. Schmell works two evenings each week while maintaining his job as a Training Manager in the Silicon Valley. He intends to leave corporate America behind once the store is able to sustain their family. "Both of us worked evenings and weekends for the first four months to learn the business and meet our customers," says Schmell. "This has been a great strategy for us."

To market the business, Costa and Schmell spread their reach across numerous platforms. They met with the city District Supervisor, Bevan Duffy, who supported the store by attending the grand opening event and introducing the business owners to valuable contacts in the area. They also launched a website, formed relationships with community news reporters, and used word of mouth to create a buzz.

Costa says, "We are not advocates of advertising in newspaper or magazine ads. We tried advertising with our merchant association and nothing came of that. We believe in having a great location for the business, direct marketing, and utilizing our network."

Even their company tag line reflects their creative energy: "Fashion for Your Sole." The thoughtful marketing strategies have contributed greatly to their success. Patrons flocked to the store for the one-year anniversary event, a catered affair complete with a service staff. To add to the appeal, they held a raffle that raised over $600 for a local charity.

"We strive to create customer delight and a reputation for great customer service," says Schmell. To add to their services and revenue streams, De La Sole places special orders for customers and even ships the products directly to the customer. They also use eBay to sell off close-out merchandise.

Investing in the right technology has proven to be a smart move for the business. "Our point of sale system allows us to keep a customer database. We ask every single customer if they would like to be on our mailing list when they make a purchase," says Schmell. As a result, the business already has a contact database in the thousands that is notified each month via e-mail about new products and sales. They also use the trend reports provided by their QuickBooks software to evaluate the busiest hours in the store and sales trends.

Now past the one-year mark, Schmell reports that shoe sales are booming and adds happily, "We are blowing away our numbers and are totally in the green." One part-time employee helps to give the entrepreneurs some occasional time off and they plan to cut back their hours in the near future.

Schmell cites a long list of key factors to success: "Learning and reading, planning ahead, staying focused on our key business and not trying to be everything to everyone, listening to our customers and figuring out what they want, learning from our vendors, keeping things simple, and being open to other people's suggestions and ideas."

As for advice for aspiring entrepreneurs, Schmell says, "I think most people are afraid of failure. But what you really need to be prepared for is success from the start, such as investing in the right tools (technology and experts) to manage your business correctly from day one."

Though there have been challenges along the way, De La Sole has put down roots in the Castro. The owners are already talking about a second location and expanding their Internet presence. "We try to have fun no matter what we do," says Costa. This positive attitude is reflected in the success of a business that was well-planned from the beginning.

Chapter 4

Options for Starting on a Budget and Creating Multiple Streams of Income

*"I can't understand why people are frightened by new ideas.
I'm frightened of the old ones."*
–John Cage

Surveys indicate that aspiring entrepreneurs are often held back from pursuing their dreams due to lack of funding. This dilemma is compounded by the knowledge that many businesses fail as a result of under capitalization. While financial limitations do make it more difficult to launch a business, there are some alternatives that can transform a dream into reality.

Consider a Phased Approach

Perhaps you dream of launching a consulting business or opening your own shop. If you're not financially or emotionally ready to take the leap, then consider how you could launch your business in phases. Here are some options:

√ Start the business after-hours while maintaining your current job.

√ Scale down your hours at your current job to part-time while devoting the rest of your time to your new business.

√ Start small and reinvest the profits into your ultimate goal. For example, if you want to open a restaurant but lack the funds, you could start a catering business on the side. This would not only allow you to build revenues, but would create some buzz around your product offering. You would even have a built-in client base when you are finally able to open your own place.

I know a business owner who launched a pool maintenance service while keeping his full-time management job at a large company—a risky move for this sole supporter of a family of five. He changed his hours at his corporate job so he could work from 5 a.m. to 2 p.m. each day, leaving him time to tend to pool customers in the afternoons and evenings. When his client base grew, he was able to negotiate part-time hours with his employer—and they even let him keep his medical benefits. A year later, hard work and persistence turned his pool service into a full-time endeavor and he resigned from corporate America for good—proving that the phased approach can be quite successful.

Do you have a first choice that doesn't seem quite attainable? Is there a second choice that could lead you where you want to go? Keep in mind that it is important to have a passion for your business. A second choice should still be a business that you will absolutely love. Running a business that does not interest or excite you increases the potential for failure.

Multiple Streams of Income

Perhaps your business idea falls short on earnings potential or requires creating multiple business entities. Or maybe you're just motivated to make a whole lot of money! Creating multiple income streams means that you have more than one source that generates revenue. For example, I earn money from my bookstore, my online business, and my writing. Many online businesses generate income from product sales, seminars, affiliate programs, and by selling advertising.

If you have more than one interest or method for generating income, prioritize them. You don't want to juggle too many balls in the air at once; however, you can implement your plan in phases.

If you are unsure whether your business idea is solid enough to make a living on its own, a second and even third income opportunity can help. There are many ways to transform ideas into profit. The topics in this chapter should provide you with plenty of ideas for branching out.

Sell a Product

Whether you have a food item, hand-made creation, artistic work, an invention or items for resale, there are numerous potential venues for selling your wares. Even better, these venues can be targeted whether your business is a part-time or full-time endeavor. Here are some options:

√ Flea markets
   √ Visit www.fleamarketguide.com or www.fleamarketeer. org for a listing of U.S. flea markets.
√ Farmer's Markets
   √ Visit www.ams.usda.gov/farmersmarkets/map.htm or www. farmersmarkets.net/visit/ for a listing of farmer's markets.
√ Auctions
√ Online auctions: www.eBay.com, http://auctions.yahoo.com/, www.ubid.com
√ Your own website
√ Local boutiques or stores
√ Trade shows
√ Catalogs (your own or someone else's)
   √ Visit www.catalogs.com or www.catalogcentral.com to locate catalogs that fit your market.
√ Giant retailers (many successful products got their start at Wal-Mart and the other big stores—check their websites for details on how to pitch your products)
√ Grocery stores
√ Wholesalers
√ Co-op markets
√ Street fairs

√ Consignment shops

√ Door to door

√ Car Wash (many of these sell gift items in the waiting area)

√ In-home parties (think of Tupperware or Mary Kay Cosmetics)

√ Corporate offices (contact human resources and arrange to set up in the cafeteria, break room or lobby)

√ Shopping channels (like QVC—check out www. qvcproductsearch.com)

√ Infomercials

√ Packaging with other products (for example, a battery tester could be distributed by a battery company)

√ Your own retail store

√ Seminars that you run (back of the room sales)

√ A rented kiosk at the mall

√ Sublet space for a shelf or a corner in a retail store

√ Craigslist online classified ads—they're free! www.craigslist. org

√ Classified ads in specialty magazines and newspapers

√ Yahoo! Stores: http://smallbusiness.yahoo.com/

Some of the venues listed above may also provide a way for you to test market your product. How much interest does it generate on eBay? What price point works best? Spend a day at the flea market and see what kind of feedback you get from the public. When selling a product, the price is just as important as the product itself. Test your product's salability by evaluating the pricing structure.

Consignment Options

Many retail operations use consignment as the foundation for the business. Consignment works by having a consumer provide an item to a merchant for sale. The merchant acts as a broker, paying the consumer a percentage for the item once it has sold.

Consigning inventory reduces the costs of starting up a business because there is no out-of-pocket expense to stock your store. This is a model that works well for all kinds of businesses. Recycled or second-hand stores are common places for consignment. Some of the types of businesses that use this model successfully include:

√ **Clothing** - Name brands and fashionable items with minimal wear can be dry cleaned and consigned in retail stores. These stores offer their shoppers quality items at a fraction of the retail cost and attract college students, corporate workers, and frugal shoppers alike. In addition to clothing, accessories like purses, belts, jewelry, and shoes can increase profits.

√ **Children's Items** - Children grow out of everything quickly—from clothing and shoes to toys and furniture, there is a solid market for used children's items. The combination of expense and necessity for these items makes them an ideal target for the used goods market. Maternity wear is another item that only receives a few months of use before its lifespan is over.

√ **Sporting Goods** - How many pieces of sporting equipment have you purchased that you subsequently used a few times—then watched as the dust gathered? Perhaps your old treadmill makes a great fixture for hanging up clothes after ironing. Many Americans have rooms filled with dusty treadmills, baseball gloves, tennis rackets, and tap dance shoes used only a few times in a passing fancy. And for every person who has a dusty stair climber taking up space, there is another hopeful person who wants to buy one.

√ **Music** - From records and CDs to guitars and saxophones, the market is ripe for used music supplies. Children may take an interest in the clarinet for a year or two, then move on to other interests—leaving parents with an expensive piece of equipment. Many parents are thrilled to find a venue to recover some of their investment for these items.

√ **Cars** - This high-margin business allows a dealer to do the selling and split the profits with the seller. For someone who wants to start a used car lot, the inventory investment is usually astronomical. But selling cars on consignment allows the owner to showcase a variety of vehicles while building up revenues.

√ *Collectibles* - The world will always be interested in collectible items, some a passing fad and some that are here to stay. Some collectible items that could be sold by consignment include antiques, books, comics, baseball cards, figurines, and plates.

√ *Furniture* - This is another expensive item that can work on a consignment basis. As people move, merge households or simply change their tastes, furniture can come and go. Selling furniture on consignment offers buyers a unique variety at an affordable price and allows sellers to recoup some of their investments.

There are many other types of items that could be consigned and sold through various forums. Traditionally they are sold at retail locations, but they could also be sold on the Internet, or at flea markets, antique malls, and other venues discussed earlier in this chapter. For entrepreneurs who are low on capital, consignment offers a chance to build a solid inventory either as the business model, or as a means to building up the capital until you can afford to purchase the inventory outright.

Sell a Service

The difference between selling a product and selling a service is that with a product, you can sell multiple widgets at a time; however, you can't perform several hours of service work in a single hour. Your time is your product which can potentially limit your earnings potential if you don't plan carefully.

When assessing whether a service business is right for you, carefully calculate your fees and the reasonable number of hours you will work. It is probably not feasible to work eight or more billable hours each day, so factor in the amount of time you won't be billing for your services—time when you are managing your business or in between clients.

It's not to say that an independent service business can't thrive. It certainly can if it is planned correctly. There are also ways to grow a service business by offering additional services or products and by adding billable staff or contractors.

Expand Your Offerings

Do you have a great idea—something you could get completely passionate about—but you don't think it can earn you a living? Consider what you can do to broaden your scope.

Example #1 – Errand Service
You would like to get paid to run errands for people in your neighborhood, but when you do the math, you can't find any way that $10 to $30 service fees could possibly add up to a decent living. Since running one personal errand at a time isn't going to work, you need to find a way to make this business profitable. Here are some ideas:

√ Offer mobile notary services and add lucrative mortgage loan document signings to your menu of services.

√ If you have a large vehicle (and insurance) market a trip or tour service to a local senior center. You could take six seniors on a trip to the bookstore, mall, theater, breakfast, bingo, etc. If you charge per person, you can increase your hourly earnings, and potentially make this a repeat service.

√ Set up a special delivery night for a large apartment complex. For example, deliver DVDs and Chinese food on Friday nights to a specific apartment building (or several of them if they are in the same vicinity). Advertise with the residents and build up the clientele so that dozens of deliveries can be made in a short time frame every week.

√ Negotiate deliveries for a local business with an hourly fee. The dry cleaner in your neighborhood may want to add delivery services. Work out a system so that you receive a fair rate for delivering clothes to customers. Other businesses that might be interested in product deliveries include pharmacies, restaurants, medical labs, real estate offices, law offices or video stores.

√ Expand your service and hire workers to run the errands. You can significantly increase the size of your business by using contractors or employees to perform the work while you manage the business.

Example #2 – Pet Sitting

You are an animal lover and know that a pet sitting service would be perfect for you, but when you do the math, it doesn't meet your lifestyle needs financially. Here are some options to expand the offerings:

√ Offer overnight pet sitting for a substantially larger fee. Many people prefer to have someone stay in their homes when they are out of town and are willing to pay for the peace of mind.

√ Subcontract other pet sitters. Make sure you get them licensed and bonded as needed, then split the profits or agree to a fee. Having a staff that performs the actual service allows you to serve more clients and leaves you more time to manage the business and focus on sales and marketing.

√ Create a catalog of pet supplies and leave one with each of your clients. Find a niche, such as organic dog treats, and make them easily accessible to your clients by offering free delivery. Your product could either consist of items you acquire from wholesalers or items you produce yourself.

√ Add additional services such as mobile dog grooming, taxi to the veterinarian, yard pick-up, obedience training, doggie day care or dog walking.

Public Speaking

It's easier than you might think to become a public speaker. Local adult education centers are always looking for new instructors. Speaker's bureaus are easy to locate and Toastmasters (www. toastmasters.org/) is a great organization for people who want to develop public speaking skills and network with others. Businesses, schools and college campuses could also provide audiences for your presentations.

The Internet has opened new doors for communications. Web seminars and Internet chats make it easy and affordable to reach audiences all over the world. Are you an expert in a particular subject? Is there a market out there for what you have to say? You could start your own website and promote your services. You can also team up with other companies and offer seminars to their clients.

Public speaking is also a great way to market a product or service. For example, local Realtors often offer free classes on home buying and selling in order to obtain new clients. Book authors speak to audiences to promote book sales, and even hypnotists conduct free seminars in order to obtain clients or sell books and CDs.

A great book to learn more about speaking professionally is *"Speak and Grow Rich"* by Dottie Walters and Lilly Walters. You can also visit the website and subscribe to the free newsletter: www.speakandgrowrich.com. You may also want to join the National Speakers Association: www.nsaspeaker.

org. More public speaking resources are available at www. businessinfoguide.com/speaking.htm.

Sell Information

People crave information and there are many products that you can produce with your expertise. There is even a new term for this type of business owner: "infopreneur". E-books and special reports are hot items in the marketplace right now. They are relatively easy to create and you only have to write the content once, yet sales can be generated for years.

If you have expertise in a particular subject, you could turn your knowledge into a profitable information product. There are literally hundreds of websites that offer resources for selling e-books, and you can also sell them from your own website. If you decide to produce and sell your own e-books, Adobe's Acrobat software (www.adobe.com) can format your books for downloading. Learn more about setting up your own website and handling sales in chapter six.

Hot Business Idea: Become an eBay Trading Assistant

EBay's online auctions have created business opportunities for thousands of people. Now the Trading Assistant program is making it easier than ever to start a business from home.

Trading assistants act as brokers, selling merchandise for others and keeping a percentage of the profits. The profit potential can be great, especially when selling high-value items.

Though there are millions of registered users on eBay, many people still don't know how to sell goods themselves. A trading assistant fills a need in the marketplace, allowing you to make a profit while helping others unload their stuff. Almost everyone has a box of items in their garage or closet that they would like to sell.

Getting Started

If you don't yet have any experience with eBay, it's easy to get started. The best way to familiarize yourself with how eBay works is to purchase some items. When you're ready to start selling, begin your spring cleaning and sell some merchandise from your home. Make sure you have a good understanding of how eBay operates before you represent your services to others.

You will need to decide what types of products you are willing to sell and may want to set a minimum value on merchandise you accept. It can be difficult to make a profit on $5 items so you may want to require that the products have a minimum estimated sales value of $10 or $20.

Most assistants set their fees at 20% to 40% of the ending auction price. You may also want to charge a per-item listing fee of $1 to $5 to ensure you make something for your efforts even if the item doesn't sell. You could opt to waive your listing fee from the commission if the auction ends successfully.

As a trading assistant, you will list the item for sale, handle all buyer questions, collect payment and shipping fees from the buyer, and ship the item. You may also need to perform some research on your customers' items to determine their estimated value. Search the closed listings to find out what similar items have sold for and list your auctions accordingly.

You should create a simple contract that your customers sign to indicate that they agree to your services and fees. You can check out the competition in your area to determine what services other trading assistants are offering and how they are structuring their fees. Check eBay's directory by zip code at http://contact.ebay.com/ws/eBayISAPI.dll?TradingAssistant&page=main.

You will also need to decide how to obtain the items from your seller. You could offer a pickup service, visit customers' homes and complete a contract there. Or you can offer a drop-off service, where customers bring their items to you. Many assistants operate from their garages so buyers don't have to enter their homes.

Promote Your Business on eBay

EBay offers a directory of trading assistants that consumers can use to locate services in their geographic area. To get listed in the official trading assistant program, eBay requires that you have a feedback rating of at least 50, have sold at least one item in the past 30 days, and maintain a satisfaction rating of 97% or higher.

A listing in the official directory is free and you can also download best practices information and other tools from eBay at http://contact.ebay.com/ws/eBayISAPI.dll?TradingAssistant&page=toolkit.

Promote Your Business

Here are some ideas for getting the word out about your trading assistant service:
√ Create a simple brochure and ask nearby businesses to display them for you.
√ Leave brochures or fliers on doorsteps in your neighborhood.

√ Place classified ads in the local newspapers.
√ Place free classified ads on www.craigslist.org.
√ Contact small business owners and offer your services to them. They may want to unload their overstock and your service could provide the perfect solution.
√ Post fliers and brochures at colleges, retirement centers, and community centers.
√ Ask your kid's school to mention your service in the newsletter.
√ Visit garage sales and flea markets and offer your services to sellers.

Launch Your Business

Make sure you follow the rules of running a home-based business and check with your county offices to apply for a business license and resale permit. Though online sales are not heavily governed, someday they will be and it is better to comply with business laws.

Also make sure to set expectations with your customers. Since many aren't familiar with how eBay works, explain the process and set realistic expectations for the final values of sales. Some may expect their items to be worth far more than they can get on eBay, and you don't want to disappoint, or worse, upset a client by selling an item for less than expected.

A trading assistant business is a great opportunity for anyone interested in a relatively easy home business. Once you launch your business, repeat customers and word of mouth should help your business grow.

Entrepreneur Profile

Jennifer Keenan Bonoff
New View Design, Inc. and The Home Business People, Inc.
Middletown, RI
www.TheHomeBusinessPeople.com, www.SportstoSchool.
com, and www.ZerotoSixFigures.com

What do you do with a Political Sciences degree from prestigious Yale University? If you're Jennifer Bonoff, you start an Internet business—and then another, and another. This Ivy-League graduate says she felt lost during her senior year at school and dreaded setting foot in the Career Services building on campus.

Following spring break, she says, "My friends and classmates were being accepted into graduate school and were accepting job offers. They were on their way to beginning life after college. I'm not claiming that this is wrong; my heart was just in a different place. I was restless. For as long as I could remember, I wanted a business of my own, but I didn't know how to get it."

Shortly after graduation, a neighbor introduced Bonoff to the direct marketing industry. "I quickly realized that this industry was not for me personally, but along the way I had the opportunity to meet many people who were involved. I saw that they needed resources to market themselves on the Internet."

Armed only with a credit card for financing—a strategy she doesn't advocate for others-Bonoff launched a business that sold gateway websites and e-mail follow-up systems to people in the direct marketing industry. Revenues grew quickly, generating between $20,000 to $30,000 per month, and Bonoff netted an impressive six-figure income in her first year. After only 18 months, she decided to sell the business to a private investor and pursue new endeavors.

She says that the most frustrating part of starting her first business was finding the information she needed. "I struggled through a lot of the process; trying to figure out how to accept credit cards online, get a website without spending a lot of money, etc."

It was this frustration that inspired her to write a book, "Zero to Six Figures." The book tells the story of how Bonoff started and grew her business, and helps readers lay the foundation for their own Internet companies.

The desire to help others also led to her next company launch. Bonoff joined forces with her husband, Doug Bonoff, and started The Home Business People. The company offers website design and business startup consulting. Two virtual employees (who work from remote locations) and one full time employee help the Bonoffs keep their business running. "I understand from personal experience the frustrations of trying to get your business up on the Internet. There is so much information out there, and so much to choose from. It can be a confusing and even expensive proposition. My goal with TheHomeBusinessPeople.com is to help you work from home by making the journey easier," says Bonoff.

A self proclaimed workaholic, Bonoff wasn't satisfied with just one Internet business. She also founded Sports to School, a website that helps high school athletes who are interested in pursuing sports in college. The business takes the opposite approach that recruiting services take by empowering the athletes to get involved in the recruiting process. "High school athletes must put themselves out there, contact college coaches, and get themselves noticed."

The athletes can set up their own websites where they can showcase their successes. They also receive a directory with access to over 20,000 college coaches for 55 sports across the

U.S. The business boasts high school clients in all 50 states and in 35 countries around the world. Bonoff says, "The fact that we are helping kids pursue their dreams of playing sports in college and offering them the opportunity to potentially earn scholarships for their abilities is very rewarding."

Though she didn't write a business plan with her first venture, Bonoff saw the error in her ways. "My limited preparation and lack of organization created problems that persisted throughout the course of my first business."

Now she writes a thorough plan for each new venture she starts and says, "You should think of your business as a long-term project. Don't feel rushed to make it happen yesterday and sacrifice the very important initial preparation."

"As for obtaining a loan—this was not an option for me. My business was truly built on a shoestring budget. I built it with a credit card and a lot of hard work!"

Much of the hard work is spent on getting attention for her companies. Bonoff is a firm believer in marketing via the Internet and credits her success to her assertive marketing efforts. "When people are surfing the Internet, I guarantee you that they will not just stumble upon your website and buy your products. You have to get people to your site." She insists that if you don't devote ample time to marketing, "your business will quickly go under."

Bonoff has written an e-Book called "100% Marketing" that details all her best Internet marketing tactics. "I truly believe that a free online newsletter is the number one most important advantage you can give yourself on the Internet. Whether you already have a home-based business, are looking to start one from scratch or have a traditional business, arming yourself with a quality online newsletter will change your bottom line forever."

Bonoff points out that with a newsletter, people must opt-in to receive your content—which means that they actually want to read what you have to say. She adds, "To put the importance of newsletters in perspective, I have made literally hundreds of thousands of dollars over the last five years directly because of the success of my online newsletters."

Distributing free information is another method Bonoff uses to promote her companies. "Getting articles published was where it all began. It was one of the very first marketing techniques that I employed with my first Internet business, and to this day I continue to have fabulous luck with it."

She says the key is to offer information of interest to your target market and include your website link. "I take time to write a well-researched and interesting article. I then spend the time to get my article published in a variety of places. Once those steps are complete, my article will continue to produce results for me over and over again. In fact, one controversial article that I wrote for my original business way back in 2000 is still being circulated around the Internet."

Her final bit of marketing advice is to strike up joint ventures with other businesses. "Every business owner is trying to generate revenues and increase profits using the assets they have at their disposal. Some have high traffic websites that can help you generate traffic for your website and others have opt-in mailing lists of potential customers for your product."

"Whenever you attempt to enter into a joint venture, make sure that you have a clear plan of what you want to do. Remember that there has to be an upside for both parties or you are not

going to make many deals. Think about what you want to get from your partner, but more importantly, think about what you are going to be able to provide for that partner."

Bonoff also shares some of her failed efforts. Investing in marketing programs like live leads, opt-in newsletter subscribers and renting e-mail lists had only fleeting success.

With two successful businesses, a book and an e-Book to her credit, Bonoff somehow manages to keep her work day to around eight or nine hours, although in the earlier years she had a hard time setting limits around her work schedule. "I was so eager to make my business work and so desperate for it to start making money that I made the commitment in my mind to completely throw myself into my business. From the very beginning I immersed myself into a 16-hour-a-day, 7-day-a-week mission. I resigned myself to the fact that if I was awake, I was going to be working."

Now she says that putting in those long hours was the biggest mistake she made and that she believes her productivity and earnings actually suffered the consequences. "Ultimately what I did was slip into a state of isolation which negatively affected my business, my mind, and my life.

"Isolation is very easy to succumb to when operating a home-based business." She realized that she missed her formerly active lifestyle and interaction with people that wasn't done through a computer or telephone. She says, "One of the best things you can do for yourself is to establish outside connections and activities from the very beginning. Maintain physical activity, join your local Chamber of Commerce, do charitable or volunteer work, join clubs or associations or take a class on an unrelated subject."

Once she realized the error of her ways, Bonoff set down guidelines and says she shuts the door to her office at the end of the business day. She even turns off the ringer to the office phone. She volunteers with an animal rescue association and has developed a social network that feeds her creativity outside of her office.

Though isolation can be the down side of operating a business at home, there are rewards that make up for it. "I have the luxury to take a day off at will and I can take a vacation at the drop of a hat." Since her business is based online, she can work from virtually anywhere. The Bonoff's take full advantage of this flexibility. "I love that we have the opportunity to spend summers in New England and the winters in sunny South Florida."

When asked what the keys to her success have been, Bonoff says she has refused to fail. "There were so many times that I could have quit because I lacked the knowledge and experience and everything seemed to be going against me. But I made the decision to build myself the type of life that I wanted, and I was determined to make it happen."

Her advice for aspiring entrepreneurs is to "go for it." She adds, "My husband, Doug, and I work with so many people each day that are looking to start a business from home, or those who have a business but need to market it more effectively. While many of these people establish great websites and succeed, there are also many who give up before they even get started."

She cites an example of a client who had a product that Bonoff calls, "Brilliant." She helped the client launch his website and he ran just one advertising campaign. When it didn't get the results he expected, he asked to have the website taken down. "He just gave up—after less than a month with a product that could have made him a ton of money if he worked at it.

"We have other clients that have tremendous ideas, get started on their websites and then disappear. Maybe they let fear get in the way."

Fear certainly hasn't been an issue for Bonoff. She has always known she would run her own business someday. "For me, starting my own business stemmed from the need to be different, the need to achieve something more. From early in my life I had the desire to be an entrepreneur. The only way I can describe this is to relate it to the desire to be a doctor. Some people just have that feeling inside them that determines their life's work."

Her political science degree may be gathering dust, but Bonoff says she is having the time of her life. "I honestly believe that all anyone needs to be successful is the courage to try and the determination to succeed."

Chapter 5

Understanding Your Business and Getting Started

"Success in business requires training and discipline and hard work. But if you're not frightened by these things, the opportunities are just as great today as they ever were."
–David Rockefeller

The following is a thorough checklist that you can use for your planning. Since every business is different, you will not necessarily complete this checklist in the order listed. However, you can use it to keep track of your progress and make sure you complete all of the relevant tasks. You might also challenge yourself by adding target completion dates to keep your plans moving forward. You can copy the list here or download a printable copy for free at: www.BusinessInfoGuide. com/startupchecklist.htm.

The Business Startup Checklist

√ ___ Determine what kind of business you want to start.
√ ___ Learn about the industry for your business.
√ ___ Analyze the market for your business.
√ ___ Study your competition.
√ ___ Educate yourself on running a business.
√ ___ Join trade associations.
√ ___ Name your business.
√ ___ Perform a trademark search.
√ ___ Register a domain name.
√ ___ Design a website.
√ ___ Obtain a logo.

√ ___ Determine business structure (sole proprietor, partnership, or corporation).

√ ___ Evaluate your personal budget.

√ ___ Write a business plan.

√ ___ Write a marketing plan.

√ ___ Locate financing.

√ ___ Create a list of startup supplies with budget.

√ ___ Set up a system for accounting and payroll.

√ ___ Apply for business license, federal tax ID, and fictitious business name.

√ ___ Select a location and set up shop.

√ ___ Order signage.

√ ___ Obtain business tools (computer, printer, fax, postage, office supplies, fixtures, etc.).

√ ___ Order business stationery (business cards, letterhead, brochures, etc.).

√ ___ Purchase inventory.

√ ___ Create operations and employee manuals.

√ ___ Hire employees.

√ ___ Set a launch date.

√ ___ Plan a grand opening event.

√ ___ Send announcements to everyone you know.

√ ___ Send press releases.

√ ___ Turn on the OPEN sign!

√ ___ Revisit your business plan and update often.

√ ___ Evaluate your marketing strategy often.

Knowledge is Key

Once you determine what kind of business you want to start, you need to learn everything you can about the industry and how to run a business. Many great business ideas fail due to lack of planning and organization. Now is your chance to thoroughly prepare your business plans for success.

Market Research

You should study the market for your business idea to make sure there is a consumer need for your product. You can pay for this information and you can also conduct some research yourself. Trade magazines may also provide some of this information absolutely free.

Start by identifying your target audience. Ask yourself who will buy your products:" Senior citizens? Teenagers? Mothers? Fathers? Parents? Other business owners? Once you have identified your target audience, go out and find them. It's best if you can talk to them face to face, but you could also cold call for information. Here are some questions to ask:

√ Have you ever used a product/service like this before? If so, what did you like or not like about your experience?
√ Would a product/service like this be beneficial to you?
√ What would you expect to pay for a product/service like this?
√ What features would you like from a product/service like this?

You can locate market information from a variety of sources:
√ Purchase industry reports from www.marketresearch.com.
√ The Harvard Business School provides consumer research: http://workingknowledge.hbs.edu/.
√ Purchase industry reports from www.bizminer.com.

Study Your Competition

Is the market saturated by businesses like yours—or is there room for a bigger, better operation? Are there absolutely no businesses like yours in the marketplace? If not, why? Is it because they have failed or do you truly have such a unique idea that nobody else in the world has thought of it yet? While this is not impossible, it is not very likely either. It is one thing to take a calculated risk, but it's another to venture into completely unchartered territory.

How can you do it better than your competition? What advantages will you offer? How will you price your services compared to theirs? Take notes on how they operate and how you will either emulate them or do something entirely different. Pick up their fliers and brochures and study their websites. Ideas are born from other ideas so don't steal from your competition, but look to them to help you build a better offering. Competition creates a healthy environment for businesses and is what drives pricing and quality.

The founders of Home Depot sought to crush their competition from the early stages. Home Depot offered products that competing stores didn't. They filled their shelves with merchandise up to the ceiling to give customers the impression that they had an overwhelming supply of products. The founders even borrowed empty cardboard boxes from their product suppliers to fill the shelves, since in the early stages they couldn't afford to buy the excess stock.

A healthy business is one that finds a market need and fills it. You will be ahead of the game if you can identify the needs of your customers and show how you can meet them. You may have designed a fantastic widget or want to offer a unique service, but you will face an up-hill climb if you have to create a need with the marketplace.

Try This:

Answer these questions in your notebook:
√ Does your business fit a need? What is that need?

√ How great is the market demand for your business? Is the market saturated by competitors or is there room for your business?

√ Who are your target customers? (age, income level, interests)

√ Where are they located?

√ How will you compete? Price, service, quality?

Pricing Your Products and Services

You will need to know what your competition is charging in order to set your pricing structure. Services can be priced hourly or by project. You can also change the competitive landscape by making your pricing seem more appealing than your competition. For example, if your competition charges by the hour, you could charge a flat rate for a project.

There is a perception of value when it comes to pricing so being the cheapest in town could actually work against you. For example, when you get a haircut, do you prefer the $10 quickie-cut or the $70 professional cut? And when you pay for the $70 cut, don't you expect a better quality of service? Consider this when pricing your services. Do you want to be the $10 dealer or the $70 dealer, or somewhere in between?

For retailers, the industry standard is to take the wholesale purchase price and double it. If you pay $2 for a widget, you then sell it for $4. If you sell it at full price, your net profit is $2. If you have a sale offering 10% off, your net profit is $1.60. Your pricing strategy directly affects your bottom line so keep this in mind later when you outline your financial projections. You will want to know how many widgets you need to sell to make a profit.

Try This:

Make a list of your top ten products or services and list the prices from each of your competitors. Use this information to price your offerings competitively.

Define Your Competitive Advantage

Master sales people know that you must be able to stand up to your competition. Take a cue from the sales industry and learn as much as you can about your competitors. Use this strategy to identify your advantages and weaknesses. It's okay if you have weaknesses, as long as you can find a way to emphasize your advantages. This will not only help you articulate your company's value to customers, but it will help you identify areas where you need to make improvements.

Try This:

List all of your competitors' key sales points and weaknesses. Next to each, describe how your company will do it better. Your answers should ultimately end up in your company brochure, on your website or as part of your regular sales pitch.

Here is an example for a used bookstore:

√ **Competition's Key Sales Points:** We have a large selection of inventory.

   Our Response: We carry thousands of books in every genre and our store is neat and organized, a trait not commonly found in used bookstores.

√ **Competition's Key Sales Points:** We accept book trades, though we'll get to them when we have time.

__Our Response:__ We accept book trades anytime during our hours of operation. We will tally credit immediately so customers can shop the same day.

√ **Competition's Key Sales Points:** We are closed on Tuesdays.

__Our Response:__ We are open 7 days per week.

√ **Competition's Key Sales Points:** Sorry, we can't check our inventory if you call with a request. Please come in the store to find what you're looking for.

__Our Response:__ We will happily check our inventory for a title and hold a book for you to pick up. You can contact us by calling or sending an e-mail.

√ **Competition's Key Sales Points:** It is a "treasure hunt" to shop in our store. We have so many books, we have to stack them on the floor! Isn't it fun?

__Our Response:__ Our aisles are free and clear. We don't believe in keeping more than two copies of any title on the shelves, which allows us to maintain a varied inventory while freeing up space so we can stay organized.

√ **Competition's Key Sales Points:** We only sell books.

__Our Response:__ We feature books by local authors, greeting cards, reading glasses, reading lights, bookmarks, puzzles, posters and other gifts. We also have a free magazine exchange.

√ **Competition's Key Sales Points:** We've been here for twenty years; our customers are loyal.

Our Response: Our customers find our friendly and prompt service refreshing.

Interview Mentors and Business Owners

Most business owners are happy to share their ups and downs and even those who aren't in your same industry can offer you some valuable advice. Make a list of everyone you know who could possibly add to your arsenal of business information. Develop a list of questions and ask for honest advice. Business owners are typically very busy, so your discussion may be best received if you offer to buy lunch. Even the wealthiest people rarely decline a free meal, and it will be worth the price of admission.

Try This:

Use these interview questions to learn from business owners.
- √ How did you launch your business? (Did you get a loan/quit your job/etc.)
- √ What was the most challenging part at the beginning of your business?
- √ What is the most challenging part of running your business today?
- √ What is the best part of running your business?
- √ What would you do differently if you started over today?
- √ What marketing strategies have worked for you?
- √ What marketing strategies have failed?
- √ How did you transition from a startup to a successful business?
- √ What do you think are the keys to your success?
- √ What advice do you have for me?

Survey Family and Friends

While it's nice to have the support of your family and friends, not everyone is going to rally for you. Some may be jealous that you are pursuing a dream they have only considered for themselves, and others may not understand your ambitions.

The people in your life who want to protect you, like your parents and siblings, may worry that your business venture will equate to a lack of security. Move past these people and seek sound advice from impartial parties.

Tell everyone who will listen about your business idea and ask them for their opinions. Do they think you have a great idea? Do they have suggestions that can help you? Do they know people who could help you? Watch for a theme. If nine out of ten people tell you that nobody is going to be willing to spend $29.95 for a widget, they might be right.

Read Business Magazines

Visit your local bookstore to find a hearty selection of business magazines. These publications are loaded with interesting articles, market trends, and business advice. Be sure to subscribe to at least one or two, and make reading them a habit. Some good titles to check out are *Entrepreneur, Inc., Fortune Small Business, Home Business Magazine, Home Business Journal, Business Opportunities Magazine,* and *Wall Street Journal.*

Locate Trade Publications

Many industries have magazines that cater to the needs of business owners in that field. Trade magazines can help you learn about the industry and locate resources like vendors and products. These are often available through trade associations and you can also locate many from www.TradePub.com.

Join a Trade Association

Find out if your industry has its own trade organization. In many cases, there may be several organizations to choose from. For example, writers have the American Society of Journalists and Authors (ASJA), the American Society of Business Publication Editors and regional associations such as the California Writer's Association and the Northern California Publishers and Authors Association.

The value of joining trade associations is often in the networking opportunities and the access to resources and special discounts. If you aren't aware of associations in your field, start asking around or look on the Internet. Evaluate the services provided by each organization and determine if the membership fee is worth the return on investment. Remember too that membership dues qualify as a business expense come tax time.

Many trade organizations are listed in the industry guides at www.BusinessInfoGuide.com. You can also locate them by searching the Internet for key words related to your industry. Enter a search combination in your favorite search engine such as Google or Yahoo!.

The following are example search combinations for locating trade organizations for a gift shop:
    GIFT TRADE ORGANIZATION
    GIFT STORE TRADE
    GIFT TRADE PUBLICATION
    GIFT TRADE SHOW
    GIFT TRADE MAGAZINE
    GIFT TRADE CATALOG
    GIFT TRADE CONFERENCE
    GIFT CATALOG
    GIFT ASSOCIATION
    SPECIALTY RETAIL

Attend Classes

The U.S. Small Business Administration offers free business classes in cities all over the U.S. Check out www.SBA.gov to find out more. The Service Corp of Retired Executives is another wonderful resource where you can obtain free one-on-one business consulting services. Visit their website at www. SCORE.org. Be sure to check your local adult education center or community college for low cost courses. Since I am one of the instructors, I am also a big fan of www.SmallBiz-Bootcamp. com.

Take Advantage of Free Internet Resources

In addition to business websites we've already discussed in this book, the Internet provides a virtually endless source of information. You can use search engines to look for information about your specific industry. Let's say, for example, that you want to start a consulting business and offer financial planning. You can use key word searches to locate trade information and articles about similar businesses. For consulting services, you could try the following search combinations:

CONSULTING SERVICE
CONSULTING SERVICE BUSINESS
START CONSULTING BUSINESS
RUN CONSULTING BUSINESS
CONSULTANTS
FINANCIAL PLANNING BUSINESS
FINANCIAL PLANNERS
FINANCIAL PLANNING SERVICE
TAX PLANNING SERVICE

If you use a search engine like Google, you can use quotation marks around a search phrase to find an exact match. For example, if you type in "START A CONSULTING BUSINESS", the search results will include only sites that contain that exact phrase. Without the quotes, the search returns results that include each word in the phrase somewhere in the site.

Most of the search engines also have an advanced search option. This can be useful for narrowing your search or omitting words from your search string. Check out these popular search engines: www.Google.com, www.Yahoo.com, and www.AltaVista.com.

Visit Online Chat and Message Boards

What better way to learn than to talk to people who are in your field? Yahoo! has an excellent selection of groups with members located all over the world. Visit www.groups.yahoo.com. Many trade associations have websites with message boards for members. This can be a great benefit of membership.

Try This:

Start brainstorming your elevator pitch. An elevator pitch is a 20 to 30 second explanation of your business and its values. The theory is that if you ever end up on an elevator with someone who is influential in your industry, you will be prepared with a pitch that will knock their socks off.

Whether or not you ever have a million dollar opportunity in an elevator, this pitch is important. You should clearly be able to explain your business to anyone you meet. This is valuable for your marketing copy, during business networking and in all kinds of business interactions.

Here is an example of my elevator pitch for my business website:

"BusinessInfoGuide.com is a directory of free resources and industry information for entrepreneurs. The site provides information on more than twenty industries including retail, food and beverage, Internet and home-based businesses, and also offers links to trade associations and resources for all fifty states."

Entrepreneur Profile

Steve Rumberg
Silicon Valley Real Estate Group, Inc.
San Jose, CA
www.SteveRumberg.com

Some people seem to be born with an entrepreneurial gene. Steve Rumberg could serve as the poster child for this phenomenon. His business savvy first appeared at the age of eight when he clipped an ad for $2.00 address labels out of the newspaper and paraded around his neighborhood offering to sell the labels for $3.00. He laughs, "The only order I ever received was from my dad's friend," but that didn't deter him. Soon he was in business mowing lawns and washing cars.

When his grandfather visited, he was so proud of the neighborhood businessman that he had some business cards printed up for Steve and his partner, Marcus. "He printed the name of the business as S&M Jobs," Rumberg says with a chuckle. "Of course I didn't see the humor in that until much later."

In junior high Rumberg ventured into candy sales. When the neighborhood drugstore offered bulk candy bars on sale, he stocked up and sold them for full price at school. He says the business was quite profitable and he carried it on through high school. In fact, when his high school business class wanted to come up with a student-run business, Rumberg suggested a candy store. The students rented soda machines, purchased candy and opened a successful shop.

While pursuing his Business Administration degree at San Jose State University, Rumberg expanded his sales offerings. He shopped at warehouse stores to acquire products and sold soda, beer, and frozen burritos from his dorm room.

Eventually Rumberg took a job at a computer store during the time when personal computers were expensive and just entering the marketplace. He taught himself how to use dBbase II and III and became the point of contact for customers who needed advice. When a client asked him to develop an inventory and accounting program, Rumberg produced a unique product that evolved into a business.

The program was tailored to art galleries and framing stores. Rumberg took his show on the road and promoted his product at industry trade shows. He found it was a tough sell. "I ended up spending more time educating people about what computers could do instead of selling the product." Though interest in computers was growing and his product was solid, Rumberg says he "made enough to eat, but it wasn't the type of income I wanted."

He eventually sold the business and took four years off to work in Japan and Switzerland as an English teacher. During the final months of his international teaching adventure, Rumberg decided to pursue his interest of working in the real estate business and began studying for a California real estate license. He returned home in 1997, passed the real estate exam and began interviewing with brokerages.

He says he realized that most of the brokerages will hire an agent simply because they can "fog a mirror." Rumberg believes that agents shouldn't have to be interviewed; instead the agents should be asking the questions. "What agents need to do is interview the brokerage and find out what kind of support they offer."

After several successful years in real estate sales, Rumberg was invited to a franchise sales presentation with Keller Williams Realty International. He attended with a large group of agents that he worked with at his current brokerage, and said that many dropped out after attending the second round of presentations. "We went from 35 people down to 20, then eventually it was down to six of us."

Six turned out to be the magic number. Rumberg and five others decided to move forward with the franchise opportunity. The team became equal partners and each invested personal income to launch their San Jose, California office. They were required to assemble a business plan and write an evaluation of their competition. The team of six formed a Sub-S Corporation and once they completed the required processes with Keller Williams, received approval and opened the first office in 2000.

Four years later, Rumberg reports that his company has over 200 real estate agents in three offices and that they are in the process of opening additional offices in neighboring cities. Overhead expenses are low because the business runs on a tight staff. They have one office manager who oversees the entire sales team, one administrative assistant who pays the bills and handles paperwork, and a receptionist.

Having a business based in the heart of the Silicon Valley makes hiring a breeze. "We've had a flood of new hires because downsized tech people think real estate sales is an easy transition," says Rumberg. "Really good people can make a lot of money with real estate but they have to be motivated to work."

One way they manage expenses is by outsourcing. "We have online backups (of data) that are encrypted and sent to L.A. Almost our entire (computer services) infrastructure is outsourced." They use a company called CI Host for their website and e-mail hosting and are pleased with the services. "My goal is to outsource everything in the company," says

Rumberg. "My advice to other entrepreneurs is to focus on what you like and outsource everything else. It's a commitment when you hire someone. But if you outsource, you can give someone a small job and see how they perform. Then give them a bigger job and so on."

If he could go back in time and do anything differently, Rumberg says he would have kept in touch with people. "Networking is really valuable and I didn't realize that until later on." He only kept in touch with a small group of friends from college and regrets that he didn't make more of an effort.

In addition to running the successful real estate office, Rumberg has expanded his business offerings to include real estate loans. He also began buying single family homes as rental properties and devised a property management system to rent out the individual rooms in the homes. This system is working so well for him that he is getting ready to launch another business: a property management company that operates under this same formula.

Though Rumberg admits that he usually works a 12-hour day, he likes the flexibility in his schedule. He also likes juggling his many projects and different businesses and says the key to success is to set goals. "People need to know what they want, set a goal and go after it."

This entrepreneur lives by his own advice and says in the next five to ten years he envisions running multiple businesses and opening even more real estate offices. "As entrepreneurs we want to be in charge, we want to set our own destiny." From lawn mowing to candy sales to real estate tycoon, Rumberg is proof that we can create our own success.

Quick Tip:

Keep a running To Do list. Do you need to update your website? Return phone calls? Contact a vendor? Remember to pick your kid up from school? A daily To Do list allows you to keep track of your tasks and prioritize them. Plus, crossing them off can give you a sense of accomplishment.

Chapter 6

Business Identity, Structure and Website

"If your success is not on your own terms, if it looks good to the world but does not feel good in your heart, it is not success at all."
—Anna Quindlen

Deciding on a business name can be a fun part of the business planning process, but should also be done with some serious thought. You could be strapped to the business name for many years to come, so you want to be sure to choose a name that you will still like in one, five or even twenty years.

You may also want to consider using a descriptive name so that it makes your business easy to identify. For example, a name like "Joe's Place" doesn't tell you anything except that a guy named Joe probably owns it. Is it a restaurant? A bar? A gift shop? If you want to include your name, "Joe's Diner" would probably be a better choice for a restaurant or "Joe's Sports Emporium" for a sporting goods store. While there are certainly plenty of companies that have thrived with non-descriptive names, your marketing efforts will be that much easier if your title makes your business intention obvious.

With that in mind, you also don't want your title to be too limiting in case your business expands in the future. For example, if you are starting a cookie business and name your business "Cookie Delights", you certainly capture your cookie audience, but what if you decide to expand to pies, cakes or other desserts? If there is a chance your business could grow in the future, you might be better off using something like "Bakery" or "Sweet Treats" in the title.

Another consideration is the cost of printing. The longer the name, the more it will cost to print signage. There can also be space restrictions for advertising and business cards, so a name like "Joe's Totally Awesome Tamales" might cause some frustration when printing your collateral.

What image do you want your business to project? Is it casual, friendly or formal? Think about the names of businesses that are similar to yours, as well as those of businesses that you would like to emulate. How do those business names get their message across?

If placement in the phone book and other directories is important to your business, you may also want to choose a name that is higher up in the alphabet. "Awesome Upholstery" is going to appear long before "Upholstery Masters."

Try This:

Make a list of key words that represent your vision for your business and try pairing up the words. Use words that represent your business values. You can use a thesaurus to come up with additional words that have a similar meaning. Check out www.thesaurus.com for a quick and easy way to search for word ideas.

Say each business name out loud, consider the phone book placement, the message that the name portrays and how they will look when printed on business cards. Does it spell out an acronym? Is it an acronym you could use?

Here is an example list for a landscaping business:

Yard Care	Service	Maintenance	Landscape	Greenery
Professional	Honest	Quick	Affordable	Complete
Thorough	Full-Service	Efficient	Dependable	Reliable
Residential	Commercial	Friendly	Custom	Unlimited

Sample Combinations:

Complete Commercial Landscaping (acronym is CCL)
Custom Commercial Landscaping
Commercial Landscaping
Lawn Care Unlimited
Yard Care Unlimited
Landscaping Unlimited
Reliable Yard Service
Dependable Yard Maintenance

Now make your own list with varying combinations. Narrow your list down to a few favorites, then survey friends and family to select the most appealing name.

Trademark Search

Depending on the size of your business now and in the future, you should verify that the business name you choose is not already trademarked. Each state has different regulations over corporation names, so if you intend to incorporate, you will need to check with the secretary of state's office to search for existing corporations with your selected business name. Even if you don't plan to incorporate right away, you could change your mind in a few years and it will be frustrating and costly to change your business name.

If you are a sole proprietor or a partnership, you will have to register a fictitious business name, which banks require in order to set up a business bank account. Fictitious business names also have to be published in a newspaper, notifying the public and allowing other business owners the opportunity to contest the name you have filed (more about fictitious business names in chapter eight). While you can use a business name that is already in use outside of your state, you cannot use it if the business name has a trademark. Infringing on a trademark is illegal and makes you vulnerable to lawsuits from the trademark owner.

Perform a free trademark search by visiting the United States Patent and Trademark Office (www.uspto.gov).

Domain Search and Website Setup

Even if your business is not Internet-based, establishing your own website adds credibility to your business and gives you another venue for locating and communicating with clients. Before you settle on your business name, make sure the domain name is available. The Internet continues to grow rapidly and many domain names with a ".com" extension are already taken. You can use ".net" or ".biz," but consider the ramifications of doing so. If a potential client types in *www.yourbusiness.com* by accident, will they find your competition?

To check if your domain is available, you can run a free search at www.smallbusiness.yahoo.com/domains. If the domain is not available, consider using an acronym or abbreviation. If the name is available and you are not yet ready to commit to hosting a website, you may want to invest in registering the domain name. It costs less than $10 and gives you ownership of the name for one year, which you can later activate and convert into an active website. When you register your domain name with Yahoo!, you also have the ability to create a single page business card with your contact information. You can keep this active until you are ready to make your website live.

If the website name you want is not available, type it into your browser to see if it is active. If not, you can check the ownership information and expiration date of the ownership by visiting www.internic.net/whois.html. If you have some time, you may want to wait for the registration to expire to see if the name becomes available, or contact the owner to see if he is willing to transfer the rights to you for a nominal fee.

There is also a web-hosting service that has a paid service that will track when a domain name becomes available and will attempt to register the domain name for you. They cannot guarantee that they can get the domain name, but if it's one you want badly enough, it might be worth the price. Visit www.godaddy.com for details.

There are many free websites available from places like Geocities (http://geocities.yahoo.com/). Just keep in mind that you will not have your own domain name or e-mail address. Instead your URL will look something like this: www.geocities.com/yourbusiness. html. If you want to establish a professional presence on the Internet, you should consider an affordable website hosting plan and your own domain name.

You can host your own website for as little as $12 per month with Yahoo! at www.smallbusiness.yahoo.com. Their starter package includes hosting and up to 25 e-mail accounts that you can set up however you like. For example, you can have yourname@yourwebsite.com, webmaster@yourwebsite.com, customerservice@yourwebsite.com, etc.

Another advantage of using Yahoo! is that you can upgrade to a Yahoo! storefront if you decide to sell products. Yahoo! also offers free site-building tools and templates that make the process relatively easy for a simple website operation.

If Yahoo! isn't for you, there are plenty of other options. Be sure to investigate the contracts with any hosting provider that you consider. You want to make sure that the domain is transferable in case you decide to switch service providers later on. You also want some guarantee of availability and data protection. This is especially important if your website generates income or plays a substantial part in your business.

Nothing can hurt an online business more than down time. If your site is down, you are effectively out of business until it is up and running again, and you could potentially lose customers. You want to make sure that your hosting provider performs regular data backups and guarantees availability. Some of the smaller hosting providers may not even back up your data, which means that if their web servers crash, you will be responsible for restoring your site.

For other hosting options, Network Solutions (www. NetworkSolutions.com) has a small business startup package for $35 per year that includes hosting and one e-mail address. The downside of having only one e-mail address is that you can't set up multiple mailboxes for customer service, sales, questions, etc. GoDaddy.com (www.GoDaddy.com) offers hosting for as little as $3.95 per month. Just be sure to weigh the value of less expensive hosting since some of these services charge for extras, like website security and traffic data (which you will want to have). A package that includes these options may be most cost effective.

Site Design

If you need help with website design, there are endless options for you. You may want to ask business owners that you know or those who have websites that you admire, for a referral to a local web designer. There are plenty of students who can do the job inexpensively, but keep in mind that they may lack the experience to know how to build an effective site. A professional website designer should infuse your pages with the right key words and optimize your site to make it easier for search engines to find you. For a professional design at a very reasonable price, check out The Home Business People (the business profiled in chapter four: www.thehomebusinesspeople.com).

If your site is mainly a big business card with a lot of static data (which is perfectly fine for many types of businesses), then hiring a designer or using a template provided by your hosting provider should be an effective solution for you.

If you have some technical skills or want to have the power to change your website contents frequently, it may be worth your time to learn how to use one of the major web design tools like Microsoft Frontpage or Dreamweaver. I personally use Frontpage and am glad that I took the time to learn how. It takes just minutes for me to add or change data on my website so I can always keep my content fresh. If you plan to make changes to the data on your website often, this is a worthy investment.

There is a bit of a learning curve with Frontpage, but you can take a class at your local college or adult learning center. I find that the tool is not always intuitive, but I can always find an answer to my questions through online help. The Frontpage Resource site offers all kinds of tips, tutorials and tricks if you get stuck: http://accessfp.net/.

Another fantastic option for those using Frontpage or Dreamweaver is to purchase a pre-designed template. Templates are also a great option for those of us who don't have a good eye for design layout. Professional templates can save you countless hours in design work. You can simply fill in your content and modify the template to fit your needs. I have used The Template

Store (www.thetemplatestore.com) with great satisfaction and success. Most of the templates cost around $20 and if you factor in the number of hours you will save in reinventing the wheel, it's a true bargain.

Website Shopping Carts and Credit Card Set-up

If you plan to sell products on your website, you will need to set up a shopping cart and the ability to accept credit cards. There are dozens of shopping cart programs available depending on your needs. You can search the Internet for shopping cart software or use one of the vendors listed here.

If your needs are basic, then Yahoo! merchant solutions (http://smallbusiness.yahoo.com/merchant/) may be a good choice for you. Yahoo! offers a shopping cart starter package for under $40 per month that includes website hosting, up to 100 e-mail accounts and all the tools to set up your shopping cart. They charge a 1.5% transaction fee for each sale under this package.

Yahoo's standard package costs about $100 per month plus a 1% transaction fee. The added features include the ability to offer coupons, sales and gift certificates. All of Yahoo's packages have the option to have your site listed in the Yahoo! Shopping directory.

To accept credit cards with Yahoo!, you can apply for a merchant account with their partner, Paymentech (www.paymentech. net/), search for your own merchant account service or set up an existing merchant account. Paymentech charges a transaction fee of $.20 plus 2.69% along with a monthly fee of $22.95.

Paypal (http://paypal.com) offers a free shopping cart setup on your existing website and allows you to process your transactions with their credit card payment system. There is no additional transaction fee other than the one used for credit card transactions. The rates for credit card transactions are based on the amount of transactions processed each month. For up to $3000 in sales, the rate is currently $.30 per transaction plus a 2.9% transaction fee. For $3000.01 - $10,000 in sales, the rate is $.30 per transaction plus a 2.5% transaction fee. PayPal's shopping cart solution is quick and easy to implement and should work well if you are selling just a few products through your site.

For a complete solution, check out 1ShoppingCart.com (www.1shoppingcart.com). This company offers shopping cart solutions, merchant card processing, auto responders for e-mail management, and the ability to set up your own affiliate program (offer others commission for sending you website traffic that results in product sales). While you can purchase all of these services individually from different providers, you would then have to integrate them and manage them all separately.

With 1ShoppingCart.com, you have the whole suite of solutions available. The basic shopping cart costs just $29 per month. The auto responder package is also $29 per month. Auto responders let you automate your e-mail responses. For example, if a customer subscribes to your newsletter, an auto responder can send a thank you message. You can also set up your auto responder to send your newsletter or messages to your customers at intervals defined by you. An auto responder system can be an invaluable tool for an active website.

For a bundling of the shopping cart and auto responder service, 1ShoppingCart.com charges $49 per month. For a full service solution that even allows you to set sale prices on your products and create your own affiliate program, you can purchase the Pro package for $79 per month. The Pro package also allows you to send e-books and electronic documents to your customers automatically.

Business Logo

Your logo is an important aspect in representing your business to customers. Business logos are a critical part of the branding strategy for big companies. Think about the logos for Nike, Microsoft and Verizon. These companies spend millions of dollars developing brand recognition so that whenever you see that famous swoosh, you think of Nike.

You'll also notice that companies strive to own a color. Who is famous for those golden arches? McDonalds, of course, and the color yellow is practically synonymous with the company name. Verizon has done an excellent job of owning black and red, while Target uses the color red and the target symbol in all of its advertising.

If your business is going to start small and stay that way, then your logo may not be as important as a company that plans to grow or wants to project a certain image. The cost of logo design can range from $200 to thousands of dollars.

The least expensive option is to hire a graphics art student to create the work for you. You can post messages at your local college or place a free ad on Craigslist (www.craigslist.org/). To commission a professional logo, you can find design services in your local phone book under Graphic Designers.

If you want to commission a designer through the Internet, check out the services offered by eLance (www.elance.com/). ELance is a directory of professional designers where you can post your project and receive bids back from the designers who want the job. Another directory of Internet designers can be found at www.allfreelancework.com. Be sure to check the portfolios of work and the credentials for the designer you hire.

There are different types of logos to consider. Some simply use the company name in a special font, such as the one used by Microsoft. Some include an image that represents what the company does or the company message, such as the target symbol used by Target. Others have an abstract representation, such as Nike's swoosh emblem.

When designing your logo, here are a few considerations to keep in mind:

√ **Colors** – The use of multiple colors will significantly drive up your printing costs on business cards, brochures and fliers. If you can keep your logo to one or two colors, you will save a lot of money in the long run.

√ **Size** – Does the image represent well in large print (on a banner) and in small print (on a business card)?

√ **Black and White** – There will be times when your advertising will be in black and white—for example, if you advertise in the newspaper. How well does your logo transfer to black and white? Make sure your designer provides you with images in black and white, also called grayscale, as well as color.

You can have your logo trademarked at the U.S. Trademark office (www.uspto.gov/) if you want to protect it from being reused. Be sure to use your logo everywhere—on your business stationery, website, store front and any correspondence. Your logo should help you create a lasting impression with your customers.

Establish a Form of Ownership

Deciding on whether or not to incorporate your business is an important decision that depends on a number of factors: how much personal liability you have in the business, how much income you generate, and how your tax payments are structured. You should consult with an accountant and/or attorney to determine the most appropriate choice. The following is a brief overview of the different business structures:

Sole Proprietor

A sole proprietor is responsible for all liabilities and debts in a business, and also receives the profits and assets generated by the business. The law views a sole proprietor and the business essentially as one and the same. It is the simplest type of business structure, though all profits are reported as personal income so there can be some disadvantages if the business makes a substantial amount of money.

IRS Forms for Sole Proprietors (visit www.irs.gov to access):
√   Form 1040: Individual Income Tax Return
√ Schedule C: Profit or Loss from Business (or Schedule C-EZ)
√ Schedule SE: Self-Employment Tax
√ Form 1040-ES: Estimated Tax for Individuals
√ Form 4562: Depreciation and Amortization
√ Form 8829: Expenses for Business Use of your Home

Partnership

A partnership can be established when two or more people share ownership of a business. In this case, the partners need to have a legal agreement drafted that defines the division of profits and assets, how much each partner will contribute in capital, how disputes will be resolved, provisions for adding additional partners and how the business should be dissolved or bought out by a partner.

A legal agreement is important because, like any relationship, not all business partners are good matches and the situation could eventually change. Similar to Sole Proprietors, partners and the business itself are viewed as one entity by the law. There are three types of partnerships:

General Partnership: A joint venture that is typically shared equally (unless otherwise stated in the legal agreement), with equal division of profits, losses and responsibilities.

Limited Partnership: This form of partnership generally specifies that the participants have limited liability and also limits the input to management decisions. This structure may not work well for service or retail businesses and is best used for bringing in investors for short term projects.

Joint Venture: This structure is used for a short term investment or project. If the partners continue working together on an ongoing basis, the structure must be changed to one of the other options.

IRS Forms for Partnerships (visit www.IRS.gov to access):
√ Form 1065: Partnership Return of Income
√ Form 1065 K-1: Partner's Share of Income, Credit, Deductions
√ Form 4562: Depreciation
√ Form 1040: Individual Income Tax Return
√ Schedule E: Supplemental Income and Loss
√ Schedule SE: Self-Employment Tax
√ Form 1040-ES: Estimated Tax for Individuals

Corporation

A corporation is its own entity that is taxed, can be sued and can enter into contractual agreements. The owners of a corporation are shareholders who elect a board of directors to oversee the major decisions and policies of the company. Since the corporation is its own entity, it can continue even when ownership changes hands.

Shareholders in corporations have less liability than sole proprietors; however, officers of the company can be held liable for legal matters such as failing to pay taxes or payroll. Corporations can deduct the cost of benefits for employees, and officers and can raise capital by selling shares of the company stock.

Incorporating requires a significant amount of paperwork and corporations must comply with federal, state, and some local agencies. Dividends that are paid to shareholders are not deductible as business income, which can result in paying higher taxes.

IRS Forms for Regular or "C" Corporations (visit www.IRS.gov to access):
√ Form 1120 or 1120-A: Corporation Income Tax Return
√ Form 1120-W: Estimated Tax for Corporation
√ Form 8109-B: Deposit Coupon
√ Form 4625: Depreciation
√ Other forms as needed for capital gains, sale of assets, alternative minimum tax, etc.

Subchapter "S" Corporation

This is a tax election that allows a shareholder to treat profits as distributions and pass through to his or her personal tax return. This means that the shareholder must be paid a salary that meets the standards of "reasonable compensation"—meaning that the wages are comparable to what would be paid to someone in a similar position. If this is not done, the IRS can reclassify the business and require the shareholder to pay taxes on all of the profits and earnings.

IRS Forms for "S" Corporations (visit www.IRS.gov to access):

√ Form 1120S: Income Tax Return for S Corporation
√ 1120S K-1: Shareholder's Share of Income, Credit, Deductions
√ Form 4625: Depreciation
√ Form 1040: Individual Income Tax Return
√ Schedule E: Supplemental Income and Loss
√ Schedule SE: Self-Employment Tax
√ Form 1040-ES: Estimated Tax for Individuals
√ Other forms as needed for capital gains, sale of assets, alternative minimum tax, etc.

Limited Liability Company (LLC)

A Limited Liability Company is a relatively new structure that bridges the gap between a general partnership and a corporation, bringing together the protection from personal liability offered by corporations and the flexibility of a partnership.

The duration of a LLC is determined when the business is filed, though it can be extended if members agree. LLCs must not have more than two of the four characteristics that define corporations: limited liability to the extent of assets; continuity of life; centralization of management; and free transferability of ownership interests.

Federal tax forms for LLCs are typically the same as the forms used for partnerships. However, if more than two of the characteristics that define a corporation exist, the business must file corporation forms.

Given the complexities, legal and tax ramifications and benefits of each business structure, it is easy to see why it is important to consult with your accountant and/or attorney when making this important business decision.

Entrepreneur Profile

Michelle Ulrich
Reflections of You, Virtual Assistant Services
Citrus Heights, CA
www.ReflectionsOfYou.com

Michelle Ulrich doesn't have to endure rush hour traffic anymore. Her commute consists of making the short trek her from her kitchen to her home office, and she wouldn't have it any other way.

After growing tired of working in corporate America, Ulrich applied for a business licences in May of 2003 and hit the ground running. Reflections of You is her growing home business where she works as a Virtual Assistant (VA).

Virtual Assistance is a relatively new industry that has opened entrepreneurial doors for men and women with office skills who want the freedom to work independently from home. The International Virtual Assistants Association (www.ivaa.org) describes the role of a VA as "an independent entrepreneur providing administrative, creative and/or technical services."

According to Ulrich, educating people on what a Virtual Assistant does is one of the biggest challenges in the industry. "A VA is not a PDA or other electronic device," she says with a chuckle. She occasionally calls herself a Business Support Specialist since many people are not yet familiar with industry terminology.

Reflections of You offers a plethora of services including graphics design, contact database management, and development and implementation of marketing campaigns. For example, clients who collect business cards each month can send them to Ulrich and she will input the data into a contact management database. She can also help a client develop a marketing strategy for an entire year. She currently utilizes the services of two sub-contractors, though all work still goes through Ulrich for final proofing and discussion with the clients.

Services are typically billed on a retainer basis. Communication with clients is conducted via e-mail, phone and fax technologies, allowing Ulrich to service customers in a variety of geographic locations. She relies heavily on her computer and software programs to accomplish tasks such as designing brochures and fliers.

*Ulrich is currently working toward her Virtual Assistant certificate through the Santa Rosa Junior College. She is also a member of California Business Education Association (*www. CBEAonline.org*) where she has delivered presentations on Virtual Assistance to educators, helping them start their own Virtual Assistant curriculum like the one Santa Rosa Junior College has had since 2000.*

*Though she is a certified Real Estate Support Specialist and says that Realtors frequently utilize the services of VAs, she has recently shifted her focus to serving business, life and personal coaches. As an active member and current Vice President of the Sacramento chapter of American Business Women's Association (*www.ABWA-Sacramento.com*), Ulrich is able to pursue her focus on professional and personal development while networking with other members and promoting her business. She rounds out her activities as a member of the International Virtual Assistants Association (*www.ivaa.org*).*

Ulrich is typically in her office from 9:00 a.m. to 3:00 p.m. four days per week and occasionally works after hours on projects. "I enjoy the flexible lifestyle that my business provides," says Ulrich. Her two daughters, ages 10 and 13, can spend time at home instead of being shuffled off to daycare.

Though she initially found that she missed the camaraderie of working in an office environment, her daily interaction with clients and colleagues has helped her adjust to working from home. She likes to play her stereo loudly and keeps her two cats close by for company. Ulrich says she mostly enjoys being her own boss and having the freedom to pick and choose her work projects.

"Ambition, persistence and just putting myself out there," is how Ulrich describes the keys to her success. She spends much of her time networking, conducting speaking engagements and working on client projects.

Ulrich plans to keep expanding and subcontracting work to other VAs while continuing her efforts to educate the public about the Virtual Assistance field. Though her business is growing, she says the greatest benefit is that it allows her to enjoy time at home with her family, creating a balanced lifestyle that she loves.

Chapter 7

Financing & Money Matters

"Money frees you from doing things you dislike. Since I dislike doing nearly everything, money is handy."
–Groucho Marx

B efore you can consider obtaining financing for your business, you need to evaluate your personal financial situation. If you plan to make a living from a business, it is important to know how much money you need to make to keep up with your current lifestyle.

Try This:

Make a list (or better yet, a spreadsheet) of your monthly expenses. Here are some items to include:

Rent/Mortgage	Dining Out
Utilities	Movies/Theater/Etc
Phone	Hobbies
Taxes	Sports/Activities
Home Insurance	Cell Phone
Auto Insurance	Pets
Health Insurance	Haircuts
Childcare	Hair Care Products
Tuition	Clothing
Groceries	Gifts
Household Supplies	Kids Entertainment
Prescriptions	Auto Maintenance
Gourmet Coffee	Gasoline
Subscriptions	Miscellaneous

Be sure to add any additional expenses not included in the list. One good way to get a handle on your expenses is to write down what you spend every day for a week or even a month. As tedious as it may seem, you will find out in a hurry where your money is going. Buying three cafe lattes per week can amount to over $500 per year!

Once you have established your monthly spending, you can begin to decide if there are areas where you can cut back on spending. Take this opportunity to evaluate your lifestyle requirements. What expenses are you unwilling to sacrifice? What is the absolute bare minimum amount of money that you need to bring home each month to survive?

It is critical that you get a good handle on your lifestyle requirements early in your planning process so that when you build your business plan, you can know whether or not your business can sustain you and how much cash you need to have tucked away until your business is profitable. Most businesses take time to build, sometimes years, and you may need to make some changes to your spending habits while you build your future.

Show Me the Money

Locating financing for your business is perhaps one of the most daunting tasks you face, but if you want your business badly enough and you put forth the effort, you should be able to find a way to fund a venture—even if that means you have to start small.

According to information provided by the U.S. Small Business Administration, Americans used several methods to fund their businesses. About 82.5 percent of small firms used some form of credit in 1998. Small firms use many different sources of capital, including their own savings, loans from family and friends, and business loans from financial institutions. Credit cards, credit lines, and vehicle loans are the most often used types of credit. Commercial banks are the leading suppliers of credit, followed by owners and finance companies.

Liquid Assets

Liquid assets are things you own that can be quickly converted to cash. While you don't want to risk your entire life savings and security on a new business venture, you do want to paint an accurate picture of where you stand. What kind of money do you have in your savings account? Do you have any stocks, bonds, inheritance funds or other sources of cash that you can tap into?

Try This:

Evaluate your liquid assets by taking an inventory of all possible sources of cash that you have available to finance your venture. You may want to make two lists: one that outlines all of your assets and another that details a portion of your assets that you are willing to invest in your business.

Savings: $_____
Stocks: $_____
Collections: $_____ (sports cards, figurines, books, etc.)
Vehicles: $_____ (weekend car, motorcycle, jet ski, etc.)
Home: $_____ (if you're planning to use home equity)
Other: $_____
Grand Total: $_____

Relatives and Friends

Relatives and friends with money are one source to consider for financing, either in the form of a loan or as a business partnership.

Be careful not to damage relationships with this option. Any financial agreements should be put in writing no matter who you are dealing with. It will make you both feel better about the exchange in the long run.

Home Equity

If you are serious about starting your business, have done your homework and feel as confident as possible about proceeding, then you may consider refinancing your home, acquiring a second mortgage or opening an equity line of credit. It is important to weigh the pros and cons of taking on this kind of debt. Can you repay it if your business fails? Can you make the payments while your business gets off the ground? Do not enter into this option lightly. There can be some tax advantages since you will be paying additional mortgage interest. And whether you take out a business loan or borrow against your home, you are still personally liable.

If you want to use home equity as a backup plan for extra funds after your business is launched, you may find it difficult to get financing in the first two years of self-employment. Without a steady paycheck under your belt, it takes time to rebuild your credit worthiness. If you think you will need to tap into your equity at some point during your venture, it might be wise to open a line of credit or pull the money out before you quit your job. Be sure to discuss all financial implications with a professional.

Money Hiding in Your House

The idea of selling off your collection of baseball cards or collectible comics may not sound very appealing, but if you really want to start your business badly enough, you will have to make some sacrifices. Take an inventory of the things you own—you might be surprised when you tally up their collective value. Consider the following types of items:

√ Antiques including furniture, figurines, fine china, or silver.
√ Collections of baseball cards, comic books, coins, or sports memorabilia.
√ Big toys such as jet skis, extra cars, and boats.
√ Miscellaneous items including board games, clothing, bicycles, tools, electronics, kids toys, furniture, and all the stuff in your garage and closets that you haven't used in more than a year.

Some venues for selling items include:
√ Garage sales
√ eBay
√ Flea Markets
√ Classified Ads
√ www.Craigslist.org (free Internet classified ads)
√ Consignment Stores
√ Pawn Shop

Financing

Small business loans are available through the U.S. Small Business Administration (SBA) and most major banks. You will need a thorough business plan and some assets (a house) to qualify for these. If you don't own a home, it will be much more difficult to obtain a loan. In this case, you might consider enlisting a partner in your venture or asking someone to co-sign.

Loans can sometimes be easier to obtain if you are buying an existing or established business, since the bank will view the investment as less of a risk. You will need to have a clean credit report when you apply for a loan. Be sure to order copies of your credit reports early so you can clear up any mistakes on your file. Mistakes are far too common on credit reports so it would be wise to check yours yearly, regardless of your situation.

The three main credit reporting agencies are:
√ Equifax: www.equifax.com/
√ Experian: www.experian.com/
√ TransUnion: www.transunion.com/

In December 2004, the SBA announced that a new bill passed by President Bush is giving their overall funding programs a boost and making $21 billion in loan financing available. This new bill also makes the SBAExpress loan program permanently available with a maximum loan amount of $350,000.

Loan Programs

The **Basic 7(a) Loan Guaranty program** is for businesses that are unable to obtain loans through standard loan programs (banks). The funds available in this program can be used for general business purposes including working capital, fixtures, leasehold improvements, and debt refinancing. The loan maturity is up to 10 years for working capital and up to 25 years for fixed assets. These loans are still delivered through commercial lending institutions, while the SBA and financial institution share the risk involved if the borrower cannot repay. There are a number of eligibility requirements, though they are broad in an effort to make this program available to as many businesses as possible. Find out more about the 7(a) program by visiting: www.sba.gov/financing/sbaloan/7a.html.

The **Certified Development Company (CDC) 504 loan program** is for small businesses requiring "brick and mortar financing." It is used for fixed asset financing, such as the purchase of real estate, buildings, and machinery or improvements such as landscaping, parking lots, and construction. Generally the assets being financed can be used as collateral. The maximum loan size is $4 million and loan maturity terms of ten and twenty years are available.

The money from a 504 loan cannot be used for debt repayment, purchasing inventory, or working capital. For more information on the 504 program, visit: www.sba.gov/financing/sbaloan/cdc504.htm. To locate a CDC location in your area, visit: www.sba.gov/gopher/Local-Information/Certified-Development-Companies/.

The **Microloan 7(m) loan program** provides short-term loans of up to $35,000 to small businesses and not-for-profit childcare centers for working capital or the purchase of fixtures and supplies. The average loan size under this program is around $10,500. Proceeds cannot be used to pay off debts or purchase real estate. The loans are funded by SBA-designated intermediaries who usually require some kind of collateral. These loans are not guaranteed by the SBA. For more information about the 7(m) program, visit: www.sba.gov/financing/sbaloan/microloans.html.

Grants

Business grants are similar to college scholarships; they are great if you can find them, but there aren't enough of them available. Grants are basically free money to fund a business, and are typically allotted for just a small portion of a business budget. Beware of scams for business grants and remember the old adage: if it seems too good to be true, it probably is. If you decide to pursue a grant service, check out its reputation with the Better Business Bureau at www.BBB.org.

Following are some resources for locating available grants:
√ A comprehensive list of grant information provided by the SBA: www.sba.gov/expanding/grants.html
√ Grant listings provided by the government: www.grants.gov
√ Private grants are listed on the Business Owners Idea Cafe website: www.businessownersideacafe.com/business_grants/index.html

Venture Capital & Other Funding Sources

Venture capital can be obtained if you can convince VC firms of your company's prosperous future. Venture funds are provided by the funding organization in exchange for equity in the company. Typically VC funding is only obtained once a business is established. Your business must have a promising future in order to garner the interest of VC firms. You will also need a solid business plan in order to begin this process.

VC Firms:
√ Investor's Circle: www.investorscircle.net/
√ Capital Across America: www.capitalacrossamerica.org/
√ GE Capital (General Electric Company): www.gecapital. com/
√ CIT Group: www.cit.com/main/default.htm
√ Crystal Ventures (for technology companies): www. crystalventurecapital.com/

VC Firms for Women-Owned Businesses:
√ Isabella Capital: www.fundisabella.com/
√ Springboard Enterprises: www.springboardenterprises.org/ about/default.asp

For a comprehensive list of VC firms by region, visit the Capital Connection website: http://capital-connection.com/vclinks. html.

An alternative to VC firms is the **Small Business Investment Companies (SBIC)** program. The SBIC program is licensed and regulated by the SBA and is comprised of privately owned investment companies that make capital available to small businesses through investments or loans. Learn more about this program by visiting: www.sba.gov/INV/.

Angel Capital

Angel investors are often wealthy business people who are interested in investing in businesses. Because they often prefer anonymity, it can be difficult to locate them. Some people place classified ads looking for angels. A good accounting office or business management consultant should be able to suggest some local contacts.

The SBA founded the Angel Capital Network which was revamped in 2004 as Active Capital. Since its inception in 1994, the network has helped entrepreneurs raise over $100 million in funding. Investors submit an application to become qualified to participate in the program. Active Capital allows entrepreneurs to be listed in their database of businesses seeking $50,000 to $5 million in capital. Visit their website for details: www. activecapital.org/.

Here are some additional sources for locating angel investors:
√ Angel Legacy: www.angellegacy.com/
√ Gathering of Angels: www.gatheringofangels.com/

Credit Cards

There are mixed opinions on whether credit cards should be used to help fund a business. The high interest combined with the high payments can compound debt quickly. But financial guru Suze Orman says that credit cards are actually a good source of business funding. Since the debt is unsecured (credit cards do not require collateral), the bank cannot take away your home if you default on payments. Credit card companies are most interested in being paid back in full and will work with you if you have trouble making payments, allowing a struggling business owner to buy some time and avoid defaulting on debt.

Orman cautions against taking cash advances on credit cards since the rates are significantly higher. Instead, she says to use the cards to acquire supplies and even inventory. Of course, be sure to choose cards with the lowest interest rates.

The Cost of Doing Business

The costs of running a business don't stop with rent, inventory and supplies; unfortunately these expenses are only the beginning. Liability insurance, worker's compensation insurance, and other employee costs must also be factored into the equation.

Small businesses are getting a bad deal when it comes to meeting the strict government compliance rules. According to information provided by the SBA, small firms with fewer than 20 employees spend a whopping *60 percent more per employee than larger firms* to comply with federal regulations. Small firms also spend *twice as much* on tax compliance as their larger counterparts.

Though there is little you can do about government regulations, it will help if you have a good handle on your operating costs and overall budget long before you even think about turning on that "Open" sign.

Start Up Supplies List

You should create a checklist of the supplies you will need for your business. Depending on the type of business you are starting, your list could be very short or overwhelmingly long. The list can be used to establish a budget and track your progress in acquiring the items you need and sticking to your budget.

Some of the types of items found on a startup supplies list include:
√ Office supplies

√ Cleaning supplies
√ Furniture
√ Fixtures
√ Shelving
√ Signage
√ Rugs and floor coverings
√ Break room supplies
√ Starting inventory
√ Shipping and postage supplies
√ Computers
√ Printers
√ Fax machines
√ Phones
√ Electronics
√ Security equipment
√ Cash registers
√ Calculators
√ Shopping bags.

Try This:

Start a list of the supplies you need and estimated costs of the items. If you have access to a spreadsheet program such as Microsoft Excel, this would be a good place to chart your progress so you can tally up the amount spent vs. your allotted budget.

To view a sample start up supplies list, visit: www. BusinessInfoGuide.com/sample-startup-supplies-list.htm.

Small Business Accounting

Record keeping is a critical function in running a small business. It would be wise to establish your procedures early so you can avoid problems later on. You can keep your own records or hire a bookkeeper or accountant to do the work for you. At the very least, you should meet with an accountant at least once during your business startup process, so you can ask the questions that are specific to your business and make sure you have access to a trusted advisor.

Monthly fees for accounting services start around $100 for small firms and increase based on the size of your business and the amount of work involved. If accounting and numbers are your weakness, it would probably be worth it to hire someone to help. If this is the case for you, ask business owners you know for a referral, or check with your chamber of commerce or trade organization for a recommendation.

If you want to keep your own books, two of the most popular software programs are Intuit's Quicken and QuickBooks: www.intuit.com/. Quicken is a simplified accounting application that is primarily intended for personal accounting, but can also be used for a very small business.

QuickBooks is a robust accounting tool that can perform everything from printing invoices and statements to creating balance sheets and running payroll. There is even a point of sale option available that allows you to transform your computer into a cash register. There are different versions of the product available with a variety of features, and the cost ranges from $100 to $3500, depending on your needs. Since the program is so robust, many business owners find it beneficial to enroll in a QuickBooks class to learn how to use the tool effectively. These are usually available at your local adult learning center, college or SBA office: www.SBA.gov.

There are plenty of books and websites available to assist you with all aspects of small business accounting. Here are some to investigate:

√ *"The Earnst and Young Tax Guide"* is published each year by one of the leading accounting firms in the country and is continually updated with new tax policies.

√ *"J.K. Lasser's Small Business Taxes: Your Complete Guide to a Better Bottom Line"* by Barbara Weltman.

√ www.taxloopholes.com/ is the site of *Rich Dad* advisor, Diane Kennedy, and provides resources for locating legal tax deductions and tax planning strategies.

Self Employment Taxes

If you are a sole proprietor and your net earnings exceed $400, you will have to file self employment taxes. Depending on your earnings, these may need to be filed quarterly to avoid penalties and the payment requirements vary depending on your industry. This is another advantage of hiring a bookkeeper since you will have a professional help you navigate these requirements and remind you when you need to file.

The IRS has a comprehensive guide for determining your requirements: www.irs.gov/pub/irs-pdf/p533.pdf.

Business Deductions

While the tax rules seem to change every year, business owners have the right to take advantage of business deductions. Be sure you save every receipt for any expense for your business. Business expenses can commonly include the following:

√ Meals or entertainment (with clients or employees)

√ Business-related travel costs

√ Mileage on your car (keep a log in your car to track your daily mileage)

√ Office supplies and any equipment or fixtures purchased for your business (some large purchases are depreciated over time for tax purposes)

√ Professional services (legal, accounting, logo design, etc.)
√ Insurance
√ Bank fees
√ Employee wages
√ Dues for professional association memberships
√ Books and educational materials
√ Advertising

If you are operating from home, you may be able to write off part of your utilities and even your mortgage. But be sure to ask your tax planner about the ramifications of writing off part of your mortgage, since there may be consequences when you later sell your house.

For additional information on business expenses, check out the Business Owner's Toolkit resources: www.toolkit.cch.com/text/ P07_2510.asp. You can also call the IRS directly to get answers to your business tax questions: 1-800-829-4933.

Payroll

If you have employees, you will need to report payroll and taxes to the appropriate authorities and withhold certain taxes from your employee's wages. Employment taxes include the following:

√ Federal income tax withholding
√ Social Security and Medicare taxes
√ Federal unemployment tax act (FUTA)

If you want to avoid all the paperwork and tracking involved in payroll (and there is a lot of it), then consider outsourcing this function. Both your bank and your accountant should offer inexpensive payroll services.

To set up this service, you will need to have an employee complete a W-4 form and then you send it to the payroll service along with wage information. Then you report the hours worked at the conclusion of each payroll period. The provider will generate the pay stub and check, or just the pay stub if you write the check. They should also run your quarterly reports and remind you when and where to send your payments.

The fees for payroll services usually include a monthly amount and a small fee for each check run. However, this can be relatively inexpensive and worth the price if keeping track of this information is more than you want to take on.

If you do decide to handle your own payroll, you will need to investigate the tax laws thoroughly. Visit the IRS guide for comprehensive information on employment taxes for small businesses: www.irs.gov/businesses/small/content/0,,id=98942,00.html

Small business tax forms, including W-4 forms, can be downloaded from the IRS: www.irs.gov/businesses/small/article/0,,id=99194,00.html. There is more information about hiring and payroll in chapter eleven.

Try This:

To Do lists can help you keep track of everything that needs to be accomplished in order to launch your business. Start your lists in a spiral notebook or binder to keep the information organized.
√ Make a list of everything in your personal life that needs to take place in order for you to start and run your business. Do you have childcare arrangements? Health insurance through your spouse? Will you have to work different hours at your business than you do now? Consider all ramifications to your personal life and how you will address them.

√ What small task can you accomplish every day to get closer to your business dreams? Make a list of small tasks such as applying for a business license, meeting with an accountant, putting your finances in order and investigating suppliers. **If you can check at least one item off the list daily, you will be well on your way.**

Entrepreneur Profile

Tammy Hitzemann
KABOOM! Retail Store
Spring Hill, FL
www.kaboomfla.com

Tammy Hitzemann knew deep down that she was destined to become an entrepreneur. She made her move when the time was right. Her popular retail shop, KABOOM!, specializes in t-shirts and accessories with rock and roll and irreverent themes, and caters to a discerning customer base of teens and seniors alike.

Hitzemann, 37, was a juvenile probation officer before becoming an eighth-grade English teacher. It was during her second year of teaching that she decided she needed a career change. She says, "Although I loved the students, the pressures of teaching, coupled with low pay and high demands, were draining."

Hitzemann decided to start a class project and challenged her students to come up with business ideas. "They all felt that there weren't enough youth-oriented businesses (in our area)," she said. "KABOOM! was a direct result of their brainstorming."

To get started with her plans, Hitzemann says she read every book, magazine, and website for entrepreneurs. She developed a startup budget that she funded with her personal savings. Though her startup budget was right on target, she says, "The continuing expense of inventory was something that surprised me. You forget that everything in the store doesn't sell all at once. There has to be a consistent flow of new and exciting merchandise, even with dead stock at hand."

To find the location for her business, Hitzemann investigated 16 empty retail spaces before signing a 12-month lease. Her husband and two sons, ages 11 and 13, along with some hired workers helped put the 600-square-foot storefront together. Hitzemann purchased retail fixtures from local hardware and discount stores and put in a lot of elbow grease herself, all while still teaching full-time.

"The last day of my teaching contract was May 29, 2004, and I opened KABOOM! on June 5. It literally meant leaving the classroom, changing into my painting clothes and working through the evening for about one month prior to opening."

To locate vendors, Hitzemann visited other retail shops, gathered information from merchandise tags and contacted vendors directly. She says, "Eventually other vendors found me, especially after attending a large trade show in Orlando."

Prior to opening, Hitzemann placed ads in several newspapers and on radio stations. "The newspapers didn't do me any good. It was a huge waste of money since my demographics listen to the radio and use the Internet." The radio promotion, she says, "was worth every penny."

To draw a crowd to opening day, Hitzemann gave away tickets to Ozzfest 2004 with the help of her ads on local radio station 98 Rock—which she credits for making the grand opening "huge!" She also asked every customer who came in how they heard about her shop, and none of them mentioned the newspaper. Since then, she has continued to rely on concert ticket giveaways and word of mouth to build her customer base.

T-shirts are the best selling items in the store and Hitzemann tries to stock as many varieties as possible. Early on she struggled with wanting to keep her store from seeming too mainstream and to keep common merchandise out of her inventory. But the reality, she admits, is that mainstream sells. "I have gotten flak from my head-bangers that think I'm 'selling out' but the truth is, the mix is better. It's better to be successful and open than trying to make a point while shutting your doors."

EBay has served as another way to keep cash flow moving. Hitzemann sells hot items and overstock on the auction site, which has the added benefit of moving old merchandise out and making room for new items. She is investigating adding a shopping cart to her own website to expand her e-commerce business.

The store is open Tuesday through Saturday for a total of 35 hours each week, though Hitzemann says she works an average of 50 hours since she has to keep up with paperwork and bookkeeping. She admits she misses spending Saturdays with her family and that it's a tough balancing act, but there are parts of the business she is able to share with her sons. "They are able to help make purchasing decisions based on what they see at their schools and their own personal preferences."

When asked what kinds of fears she faced when starting her business, Hitzemann answers, "What kind of fears didn't I face? I was afraid of losing all of my savings on this venture, failing miserably, and having to eat a lot of crow until I found another job. There were many sleepless nights over the decision to be my own boss. I have always been independent financially, and wondered if a paycheck was something I could live without."

Hitzemann says her husband and sons have always been 100% supportive, but not everyone liked her business idea. "My extended family never agreed with the business, due to the irreverent themed items. The 'F Bomb' isn't something everyone is comfortable with, my siblings included."

Though she never sought a mentor, Hitzemann said she was more interested in talking to people whose businesses had failed. She says, "I wanted to know the pitfalls and make sure I was really ready. Many of them were full of great advice." The common theme from the discussions: cash flow problems. "That seemed to be the number-one reason for failure—not enough money from the start."

Having enough cash reserves kept KABOOM! afloat during the back-to-back hurricanes that struck Florida in 2004. "If I hadn't had the money, I would have really struggled. People weren't into buying a silly t-shirt when life supplies were needed."

If she had to do it all over again, Hitzemann says, "I would have gotten over myself when it came to mainstream ideas. I also would have copied more of the stores that I liked. I forgot that I was here to make money, not a statement!" She credits listening to her customers and meeting their needs as being her primary strategy for success.

"I think a true entrepreneur always struggles with having a boss," says Hitzemann. "Most of us then come to the conclusion that we need to branch out on our own."

Hitzemann advises that aspiring entrepreneurs try to ignore the negative comments from people who try to talk you out of pursuing your goals. "If you have done your research, and are ready to roll, brush yourself off and begin your adventure! Hey, you only live once."

Chapter

8 Licensing & Insurance

"There's no secret about success. Did you ever know a successful man who didn't tell you about it?"
—Kin Hubbard

There are a number of different licensing requirements for businesses that depend on where you live and the type of business you operate. Some businesses may also have unique insurance needs so it's important to understand what the requirements are.

Business License

Every state, city and county has different regulations for general business licenses. A business license allows you to comply with your area business requirements. The fees range from $50 to $300 and are renewed each year. Each state also offers assistance for starting up a business and meeting regulatory requirements. Be sure to take advantage of all of the free resources available in your area.

Certain types of businesses may also be required to apply for special business licenses. For example, businesses dealing with alcoholic beverages, firearms, used goods or adult entertainment may require special license approval. These licenses can also take longer to be issued, sometimes up to three months, so be sure to apply early.

Business License Resources by State

Alabama: www.ador.state.al.us/licenses/authrity.html
Alaska: www.dced.state.ak.us/occ/buslic.htm

Arizona: www.revenue.state.az.us/license.htm

Arkansas: www.state.ar.us/online_business.php

California: www.calgold.ca.gov/

Colorado: www.state.co.us/gov_dir/obd/blid.htm

Connecticut: www.state.ct.us/

Delaware: www.state.de.us/revenue/obt/obtmain.htm

District of Columbia: www.dcra.dc.gov/

Florida: http://sun6.dms.state.fl.us/dor/businesses/

Georgia: www.sos.state.ga.us/corporations/regforms.htm

Hawaii: www.hawaii.gov/dbedt/start/starting.html

Idaho: www.idoc.state.id.us/Pages/BUSINESSPAGE.html

Illinois: www.sos.state.il.us/departments/business_services/
  business.html

Indiana: www.state.in.us/sic/owners/ia.html

Iowa: www.iowasmart.com/blic/

Kansas: www.accesskansas.org/businesscenter/index.
  html?link=start

Kentucky: www.thinkkentucky.com/kyedc/ebpermits.asp

Louisiana: www.sec.state.la.us/comm/fss/fss-index.htm

Maine: www.econdevmaine.com/biz-develop.htm

Maryland: www.dllr.state.md.us/

Massachusetts: www.state.ma.us/sec/cor/coridx.htm

Michigan: http://medc.michigan.org/services/startups/index2.
  asp

Minnesota: www.dted.state.mn.uss

Mississippi: www.olemiss.edu/depts/mssbdc/going_intobus.
  html

Missouri: www.ded.state.mo.us/business/businesscenter/

Montana: www.state.mt.us/sos/biz.htm

Nebraska: www.nebraska.gov/business/html/337/index.phtml

New Hampshire: www.nhsbdc.org/startup.htm

New Jersey: www.state.nj.us/njbiz/s_lic_and_cert.shtml

New York: www.dos.state.ny.us/lcns/licensing.html

New Mexico: http://edd.state.nm.us/NMBUSINESS/

Nevada: www.nv.gov

North Carolina: www.secstate.state.nc.us/secstate/blio/default.
htm
North Dakota: www.state.nd.us/sec/
Ohio: www.state.oh.us/sos/business_services_information.htm
Oklahoma: www.okonestop.com/
Oregon: www.filinginoregon.com
Pennsylvania: www.paopenforbusiness.state.pa.us
Rhode Island: www.corps.state.ri.us/firststop/index.asp
South Carolina: www.state.sd.us/STATE/sitecategory.
cfm?mp=Licenses/Occupations
South Dakota: www.sd.gov/Main_Login.asp
Tennessee: www.state.tn.us/ecd/res_guide.htm
Texas: www.tded.state.tx.us/guide/
Utah: www.commerce.state.ut.us/web/commerce/admin/licen.
htm
Vermont: www.sec.state.vt.us/
Virginia: www.dba.state.va.us/licenses/
Washington: www.wa.gov/dol/bpd/limsnet.htm
West Virginia: www.state.wv.us/taxrev/busreg.html
Wisconsin: www.wdfi.org/corporations/forms/
Wyoming: http://soswy.state.wy.us/corporat/corporat.htm

Additional Resources:

√ The IRS also offers links to every state with multiple
business resources: www.irs.gov/businesses/small/article/
0,,id=99021,00.html
√ More resources by region can be found at: www.
BusinessInfoGuide.com/regional.htm
√ Business.gov provides legal and regulatory information to
small businesses in the U.S. This site is loaded with excellent
information for every state to help entrepreneurs find answers
and resolve problems and can be found at: www.Business.
gov.

Federal Tax ID

A federal tax ID, also known as an Employer Identification Number (EIN), is used for tax reporting purposes. You need a federal tax ID number if you have one or more employees on a payroll or if you form a corporation. Sole proprietors without employees can usually use their social security number for tax reporting and are not required to apply for a federal ID (though you can still apply for one if you don't want to use your Social Security number). Visit www.irs.gov/businesses/small/article/0,,id=98350,00.html for more information or to apply using form SS-4.

Resale Certificate

If your business sells taxable goods, you will need to apply for a resale license. A resale license will be needed if you purchase from wholesalers, allowing you to buy your merchandise without paying sales tax, which also means that you are responsible for collecting taxes when you make a sale. Each state and local authority has different requirements for tax rates, collection and reporting methods. The Business Owner's Tool Kit website has an excellent directory of tax requirements for each state: www.toolkit.cch.com/text/P07_4500.asp.

Fictitious Business Name

Sole proprietors and partnerships must file a fictitious business name statement when operating a business under any other name other than that of the owners. These are filed at the county level and you will receive instructions when you file for your business license. You will likely be asked for this document when you apply for a business bank account so that you can accept payments to either your business name or your personal name.

Business Insurance

Business insurance is an entirely different animal from the personal auto and home insurance that you probably already carry. Not all agents deal in business insurance. Your trade organization may provide a recommendation for insurance providers. This can be particularly helpful in certain high-risk industries, since you know in advance that the insurance provider understands what your business is all about. You can also talk to the insurance agent that handles your home owners or auto policy. If she doesn't sell liability insurance, she should be able to refer you to someone who does.

Liability Insurance

Liability insurance protects you from lawsuits or liabilities filed by customers or employees. If a customer slips and falls in your place of business, your insurance policy should cover the damages. If you are ever the target of a frivolous lawsuit, your insurance policy should take care of the legal fees and litigations. Not all policies are created equal, however, so be sure to check the details of any policy that you consider.

If you are going to lease a commercial location for your business, your landlord will probably require proof of liability insurance. Since the fees for this type of insurance can vary, it is a good idea to get some quotes early on and build this expense into your budget.

Liability insurance is becoming increasingly more difficult to obtain as frivolous lawsuits increase and the rest of us are penalized. You may even need to provide a business plan to the insurance agent in order to convince the insurer that you are a good bet. For certain industries, liability insurance can be even more complicated or expensive if the chances of an accident happening are higher (if you serve alcohol, for example).

Property Coverage

In the event of a disaster (a water pipe breaks and floods your building) or other property damage, property coverage can protect you from losses. Fixed property insurance should cover the building itself and can also cover the contents such as fixtures and inventory. If you are renting the building, the property owner probably carries some level of insurance. You should ask what is covered in his policy. When in doubt, it is always best to carry your own policy.

Worker's Compensation Insurance

Many states now require that companies with employees carry worker's compensation insurance. This type of policy covers damages resulting from employee injuries. It is relatively expensive in some states (like California) so it would be wise to factor this into your plan early. Check the state listings provided in this chapter to find out if your area requires that you carry worker's comp insurance.

Commercial Auto Insurance

If you have a company vehicle or a business that makes deliveries, you will need a commercial auto policy. These policies can include coverage for collisions, comprehensive, rental cars, and towing. Also check your existing coverage of vehicles for both you and your employees (if applicable) since personal auto insurance does not always cover claims that occur during business operation.

Additional Resources:

There is a comprehensive list of business insurance providers for each state available at www.InsuranceFinder.com. Be sure to research your insurance needs early so you aren't hit with any surprises later on.

Entrepreneur Profile

Desalene Jones
Cha Cha's Doggie Daycare
Sacramento, CA
www.chachasdaycare.com

Dogs of all shapes and sizes get the royal treatment at the popular canine retreat, Cha Cha's Doggie Daycare in Sacramento. Owner Desalene Jones took her love for pooches and transformed her home into a haven for her furry friends, proving to her doubters that she could make money doing something she loved.

Jones, 33, holds a B.A. in public relations and spent several years working in various customer service roles. She says, "Customer service is such a draining position to be in. People yell and curse at you all day long and you are expected to accept their behavior with a smile and not take it personally." Jones spent a lot of time wishing she could bring her dog to work and even tried to get a program launched at her office. But it never came to fruition. Eventually she began to consider her options.

"I just couldn't take one more person unleashing their bad day on me," said Jones. "Finally I decided that my happiness was important enough to risk it all." She started by reading, taking some classes through the SBA, and writing a business plan. "I didn't really have a startup budget per se. I knew how much money I had in savings, which was basically nothing, and worked with that as long as I could."

Outside support for her business pursuits received varied reactions. "My mom thought it was a great idea. A few friends humored me; everyone else thought I was nuts and would fall flat on my face."

*Jones admits that nearly everything cost more than she antici-
pated—a common issue for new entrepreneurs. When funds ran
low, she turned to* www.count-me-in.org, *an organization that
helps women business owners locate business loans. She says,
"They have been really helpful with (locating) loan money."*

*She initially launched her business as a pet-sitting service, going
to people's homes to care for their animals while they were away.
Jones says that she realized that her heart was with dogs, not
necessarily all animals, and decided to refocus her business and
bring dogs into her home.*

*In order to prepare for her new furry clients, Jones had to install
rubber floors and secure all exits to keep the dogs in the front
area of her house. Her front door opens into a small foyer with
a gate to separate visitors from the dogs at play in the front
room.*

*The primary offering at Cha Cha's is daily daycare, where dogs
are entertained throughout the day and even participate in nap
time. Jones also hosts doggie birthday parties, provides obedience
training and offers weight loss camp for chubby puppies. The
majority of the revenues come from slumber parties (dogs that
spend the night) and monthly daycare packages. All new clients
are interviewed and evaluated on their ability to play well with
others. They must also be spayed or neutered and vaccinated.*

*A typical day for Jones involves an exhaustive list of tasks:
feed dogs breakfast, pick up dog beds, poop-scoop, check the
schedule to see who is coming, check staff schedule, return calls,
book new dogs coming in, greet clients as they arrive, start
laundry (a non-stop chore), assign tasks to staff, separate dogs
into appropriate play groups, check vaccinations, organize field
trip locations, talk with vendors, respond to e-mail, update the*

website, relieve staff for lunches and breaks, schedule new client interviews, run to the bank, and pick up supplies.

Marketing her business brings its own challenges. Jones praises word of mouth as the best form of advertising. "I have a fairly unique business so I send out press releases to the local media and publications." These efforts have resulted in several news stories about her daycare center. She also advertises through direct mail and says, "Door hangers are nice reminder form of marketing. People keep them in a junk drawer and pull them out when they need me." Yellow pages ads, she says, haven't worked for her.

Finding good reliable staff is an ongoing issue for Jones, who currently has four employees. "I am still working on this issue and am always prepared to do it alone again if I have to." The long hours also take their toll. "I have a 24-hour-a-day business and finally, in my fifth year, I'm closed on Sundays. However, just because I'm closed to human clients doesn't mean I don't have my 4-legged buddies around, and paperwork and all the other stuff that comes with owning your own place."

Since launching her business in 2000, Jones says she has faced many challenges. "Of course I worried I would fail and be broke and homeless. I worried that I would never get funding… I worried that I would never find good staff." Yet even with all of her concerns, Jones has found a way to overcome every obstacle.

Jones credits positive thinking as the secret to her success. Her favorite resources for entrepreneurs include the SBA (www. sba.org), "Business By the Book" by Larry Burkett and "Today Matters" by John C. Maxwell.

If she could do anything differently, Jones would "probably take the easier route and buy an established dog daycare." She has plans to expand her business and open additional locations. "There are others out there who would like to own their own businesses, but can't go through all that I did to make it happen. I would like to help those people by offering my expertise and business name."

Jones is proof that you can turn a passion into a thriving business. "I love what I do," she says, "and I cannot wait to assist someone else in realizing their dreams."

Chapter 9

Location, Vendors & Setting Up Shop

"Success is not the result of spontaneous combustion.
You must set yourself on fire."
—Reggie Leach

Deciding where to locate your business affects your bottom line and all of your planning. Will you run the business in the city where you live? Or will you be moving to accommodate it? Will you rent an office, warehouse or retail space or will you work from home? Will this space meet your needs in one, three, five or ten years?

Home Based Business – Pros and Cons

According to a federal report released by the Department of Advocacy of the U.S. Small Business Administration, home businesses now make up 53% of the small business population. If this is an option you are considering, be sure to weigh the pros and cons carefully.

Logistics

While the idea of working at home in your pajamas can be alluring, some people find it doesn't meet their expectations. If you have family at home, the interruptions could affect your business and your family relationships negatively. Others find it can be lonely to work from home. If you are a "people person," you might find it difficult to adjust to the solitary lifestyle, though some home workers compensate by socializing during non-work hours.

Home business owners also need to be self-motivated. Without a boss to oversee your work habits, it can be tempting to surf the Internet for an hour, flip on Oprah, clean the kitchen or do a couple of loads of laundry. When you start throwing in extra household tasks, they can add up quickly and suck up your valuable work time.

If you have never worked from home before, see if there is a way you can do a trial run before you gamble on it and find out it doesn't suit you. Would your current job allow you to work from home one or two days each week? If not, use your business planning efforts to emulate working from home. Spend a Saturday "at work." Treat it like a work day and spend time on your business plan or other activities. See if you are easily distracted. Ask your family to ignore you for the day. Are you lonely? Do they interrupt you anyway? Will this be an ongoing problem?

Some people find that they are very productive when working from home, and that one of the primary keys to success is to have a functional home office. If you are working from your kitchen table amidst a sea of distractions, you are setting yourself up for disappointment. But if you have a designated office space with a comfortable chair and desk, working from home may be a great choice for you.

If you are going to have to meet with clients, you will need to decide if you are comfortable having them come into your home. One option is to use a local coffee shop as a meeting location, but some clients may be turned off by this. Your other option is to go to your clients and meet them at their homes or place of business. Again, be sure to weigh the professionalism of this practice. If you are a freelance writer, most people will expect you to work from home. Many bookkeepers also work from home, but larger companies may prefer to work with someone who has a commercial office location.

Financials

The IRS has strict rules about home business deductions; however, there can be many advantages come tax time. Talk to your accountant to find out what will work best for you and what deductions you can take. In many cases, you can deduct the furniture and supplies used to furnish your home office, though some are amortized over several years.

Working from home could also save you money on dry cleaning, lunches out, business attire, and auto expenses if you don't have to commute.

Keys to Success

Your home office needs to be a functional, comfortable place for business. We've all heard stories about businesses that started from the dining room table or in the corner of a bedroom, but it's best to have a real office if possible. If you take your business seriously, others will too. Set up a professional office, even if you have to place a discarded door across two filing cabinets—at least you will have a designated space that is functional for your needs. Include all of the office equipment that your plan can afford. If you are going to spend half your time driving to the copy center for faxes and copies, you may find it makes more financial sense to have your own machines.

Also, be sure you have a comfortable chair. This may not seem like a priority, but if you start a business, you will probably spend 8 to12 hours each day in that chair. Invest in one that you love and one that is good on your back. Many of the office supply stores rate the chairs based on the level of comfort for a specified number of hours. Some expensive executive chairs are only recommended for four hours per day, so be sure to read the ratings.

Zoning Restrictions

Every county is different and has its own rules for businesses, both residential and commercial. Check with your county's business office to be sure that your type of business is allowed to operate at home. Some counties limit the number of people that can come and go from a residential business each day. They also limit the quantity and types of products that can be sold. This is an important step that you should take early in your planning process. You don't want to base your entire plan on a home-based business only to find out that you aren't allowed to run it in your area.

Commercial Office and Retail Space – Pros and Cons

When it comes to leasing space, I strongly suggest enlisting some professional help. Too many business owners take this on themselves and end up frustrated in the process. While there are "For Lease" signs posted on buildings across America with phone numbers that make it easy to simply dial from your cell phone when you drive by, this is not the best way to go. Find a commercial Realtor—a good one that you like and respect—and have them assist you in finding a space and negotiating your lease.

Without your own representation, you will deal with the Realtor or property manager that represents the property owner and you will have to look out for your own best interests. If you have a strong personality or a sales background, this may not seem like a major obstacle, but you will be dealing with all new terminology, conditions, and contracts you have never encountered before.

In most cases, your Realtor shouldn't charge you a fee. Her fees should be paid by the property owner upon closing so it will cost you nothing to have the benefit of her expertise. A good Realtor has the advantage of experience and can tell you the pros and cons of different neighborhoods and buildings. While you should ultimately decide what you are willing to negotiate, a professional Realtor will handle the negotiations and will help you review the contract details.

Location

For many businesses, the location can be as important as the product. If you are opening a retail store, you will probably want to place yourself in an area where there is substantial foot traffic. However, if you are a destination store (a place people go for a specific need even if it is out of the way), such as a stereo repair shop or comic book store, location may not be as important.

If foot traffic is important to your business, then you will want to be located near an "anchor" store, such as a grocery or department store. Of course these locations are going to be significantly more expensive as a result. Compare the prices of the big shopping centers in your area with the smaller strip malls. Many business owners end up regretting setting up shop in the smaller centers because the money saved in rent has to be spent on advertising to make up for the lack of foot traffic. But if your budget doesn't allow for the anchored shopping center, you may have little choice.

One way to determine your best location is to examine where your competition is located. Are your competitors thriving in less desirable locations? Or have you seen your competitors close up shop in those locations?

If you are seeking office space, you also have numerous choices. Who are your clients and what image do you want to project? Will your clients visit your office? If so, then it needs to be a building that meets the image you want to portray. If your clients are remote and will rarely if ever visit you in person, then you can probably afford to rent a less expensive space in a building with few amenities.

With any commercial space, be sure to consider parking availability and public transportation. Make sure the location is accessible and in a safe area. If you look in neighborhoods you aren't familiar with, visit the location after hours. How many cars are in the parking lot? What kinds of people are looming? You wouldn't want to open a coffee shop only to find out that your best foot traffic comes from the homeless community.

Finding the right location requires patience and diligence. You want to set up shop far enough away from the competition, while finding a space that meets your needs and doesn't send your budget through the roof. You will most likely have to make some compromises along the way.

Financials

The rules for commercial rentals are far different from those when renting an apartment. While every place is different, in most cases the landlord will take very little responsibility for the space once your lease begins. That means you could be responsible for the majority of the building maintenance and repairs—though your lease will spell out exactly what you are and are not responsible for. If your water heater or air conditioner breaks, you will likely have to pay for the repairs.

Rental rates are typically based on square footage. Rates can vary dramatically depending on geographic location and the existing businesses near the location. Buildings in large, expensive cities have far higher rental rates than those in small, urban areas. Buildings that are in popular shopping centers with anchor stores are more expensive than buildings that are off the beaten path.

When looking for a space for your business, determine how much space you need and what other requirements you have. Do you need to have one or more bathrooms? A kitchen or a special sink? How much storage space will you require? Will the space allow your business to grow over the term of the lease?

Try This:

Make a checklist and take this with you when you evaluate locations. After you look at several spaces, it will be easy to confuse the pros and cons of each location, so do yourself a favor and take notes. Here is an outline for an assessment that you can recreate:

Location Assessment

√ Name of building/shopping center:
√ Address:
√ Freeway access:
√ Public transit access:
√ Parking availability, cost and proximity:
√ Agent info:
√ Square footage:
√ Price:
√ Utilities included:
√ Nearby businesses:
√ Foot traffic?
√ Street visibility?
√ Average operating hours of neighboring businesses:
√ Central heat?

√ Central air?
√ Wired for security?
√ Proximity to nearest competition:
√ Storage area size and description:
√ Bathroom(s) detail:
√ Kitchen area detail:
√ Back office?
√ Color and condition of carpets:
√ Any fixtures included?
√ Repairs needed:
√ Other details:

Zoning

Be sure to check on the zoning requirements for your business. Depending on the type of business, there may be special requirements for where it can be located. For example, certain types of businesses can't be located near a school. Businesses that serve food usually need to have special sinks installed to meet health department standards.

Signing a Lease

A commercial lease will likely be long and detailed and should be reviewed with great care. The best option is to have a lawyer review it. At the very least, you should have your Realtor assist you and explain the terminology and the terms.

You shouldn't have to accept a lease at face value. In most cases, the landlord expects to make revisions. Ask questions about the terms you don't understand and decide what is most important to you. Don't over commit. If your business plan is only for three years and you think you might want to sell or expand after that time, then don't sign a five-year lease (they will always attempt to lock you in for the longest possible time).

The landlord is going to try to get the best deal possible, so it's up to you to negotiate a better deal. If improvements need to be made to the building, and the landlord leaves you with this task, then it is perfectly reasonable to request free rent in return. In fact, most landlords expect to offer at least one or two months of free rent to allow you time to set up shop.

You may have more bargaining power if the space has been empty for awhile and you know the landlord is eager to rent it out. In this case, ask for additional months at half the normal rental fee. The landlord is a business owner too and worries about cash flow just as you do. If you offer to pay six months at half rent, you will essentially receive three months of free rent. What about asking for the entire first year at half rent while you establish your business? For anxious landlords, this creates a win-win situation since the landlord is still collecting some amount of rent each month while giving you an opportunity to establish your business.

Own the Store

Depending on your financial situation, you may want to consider buying the building where your business will be located. One option is to buy a building with existing tenants who pay enough rent to cover the mortgage, while leaving you enough space to operate your business. Like all businesses, be sure to look for properties that have the proper zoning for your type of business. Commercial real estate has tax advantages and disadvantages, so discuss this option with your accountant before proceeding.

Sublet Space

Subletting space is one way to manage costs while meeting the needs of a business. Many existing businesses have space to spare and are willing to rent the space for a nominal fee. For example, an office building with empty offices or conference rooms could provide a comfortable office space for someone who doesn't want to work from home yet doesn't want to lease an entire office. As with any lease agreement, evaluate your needs and the terms carefully. Will a month-to-month agreement provide you with enough stability? Can the landlord commit to a long-term arrangement? If the arrangement is only temporary, you may end up having to reprint your business stationary or renting a post office box.

For food-related businesses, renting time in a commercial kitchen can dramatically reduce the costs of launching the business. There are many regulations surrounding the food service industry and food providers are often required to work from a commercial kitchen. If you can't afford an entire space of your own, consider renting time in the kitchen of your local church, community center, school or even bakery. As long as the hours you keep don't coincide with their hours, you should be able to reach a reasonable agreement. Check with your local health department to verify their requirements before you select your location.

Additional Resources

Check your local newspapers for commercial real estate and Realtor listings. Individual real estate firms often have listings on their websites so check your favorite firms for listings. Here are two online resources to get you started: www.LoopNet.com and www.realestate.yahoo.com.

Wholesale Suppliers

Finding suppliers can be a daunting challenge for new business owners. Even if you are in the planning or consideration phase, you should begin to investigate your options and compile a list of suppliers. You can order catalogs and start to learn what kind of buying terms are available. This will also be essential in building your estimated cost of inventory.

Keep location in mind when purchasing inventory. While you will want to compare prices of comparable items, you should factor in the cost of shipping. Shipping items across the country will cost more than shipping across the state. And shipping from outside of the country could have its own pricing and import rules. Don't skimp on research when it comes to selecting your trusted suppliers.

Quantity discounts are almost always available and many whole-salers will bait you with deep discounts for large purchases. Determine how much inventory you can reasonably afford to store—that big discount won't be worth it in the long run if you use up half of your storage space for a year trying to accommo-date your hefty purchase.

Most wholesalers offer credit terms such as net 30 (payment due within thirty days). The problem is that most won't extend terms to new businesses until you establish your credit worthiness— the typical catch 22. You will be asked to provide three or four references of suppliers who have extended you credit terms and it may take months to acquire these references. As a result, you will probably have to pay up front for initial purchases. Ask about the supplier's credit terms and learn what is involved in establishing credit. Everything is negotiable, so after placing several orders, ask for them to extend you a small credit line even if you can't provide all the required references yet. Your smaller suppliers will probably comply.

Many vendors have a minimum purchase amount and these can vary greatly. If one vendor has a minimum purchase amount of $500 while a similar vendor doesn't have any minimum purchase amount but their prices are just slightly higher, it may make better financial sense to order from the more flexible supplier. When you run low on one item from the supplier, but don't yet have a need to place a large order, the more flexible supplier could help you manage your cash flow.

Do Your Homework

Be sure to research the companies that you want to do business with. You can check the Better Business Bureau (www.BBB. org) for complaints against a company. Hoovers (www.Hoovers. com) is a good resource for learning basic company information. It never hurts to enter a company name in a Google search to see what kinds of articles or discussions on message boards show up.

Depending on the products you will carry, you may have a myriad of suppliers to choose from. If this is the case, be sure to interview each before placing an order. Here are some questions to ask:
√ Where are products shipped from? (This is an important factor when calculating shipping rates.)
√ How long have you been in business?
√ What businesses do you service in my area?
√ Do you have a sales representative in my area who can meet with me?
√ Do you have a minimum order amount? What is it?
√ How are shipping fees calculated?
√ Do you offer free shipping on orders over a certain amount?
√ What are your payment terms?
√ How do I establish credit with your company?
√ What are your policies on product returns?

You should also make a list of the products you would order from this supplier and in what quantities you are required to order. Some may ship individual products, while others may require that you order by the case. If you complete this process for several vendors, you can compare the policies side by side. This should give you a clear idea of which supplier will best meet your business needs.

Locating Suppliers

The Thomas Register (www.thomasregister.com) is the leading industry database of vendors. The following are some additional ways to locate suppliers.

√ *Basic Internet Searches*

Thank goodness for the power of the Internet. You should be able to locate many suppliers using key word searches for your industry and products. Once you locate suppliers that look interesting, sign up for their catalogs and mailing lists. Here are some examples of search terms for a sporting goods store:
- Wholesale sporting goods
- Wholesale (insert sport)
- Sports supplies
- Wholesale sports
- Wholesale sportswear
- (insert sport) supplies
- Wholesale (insert supplies)
- Resell sporting goods
- Sporting goods outlet
- Sports supplier
- Sports overstock
- Sports liquidator

Be creative with your search strategy. Identify keywords specific to your inventory and try many combinations until you find exactly what you need.

√ *Trade Organizations and Trade Shows*

Trade associations often list suppliers on their websites, at their trade shows and conferences or in their newsletters and magazines. See chapter five for information on locating your trade associations.

Trade shows create wonderful opportunities for locating suppliers and seeing merchandise in person. Visit The Ultimate Tradeshow Network at www.tsnn.com/ or Trade Show Week: www.tradeshowweek.com/.

√ *Suppliers By Brand*

If you are planning any kind of retail operation, it is likely you have some specific brands in mind. You can search the Internet for the brand name to locate a supplier. Most businesses have an Internet presence so you should be able to locate nearly any product.

You may also want to start looking at similar businesses to find products that you like and would like your business to carry. I stock gift items and greeting cards at my bookstore and I've found many by shopping in other stores all over the country. Whenever I come across a unique item, I buy it and then contact the vendor listed on the product. Product labels often indicate the parent company name or even the web address.

You can also ask store owners to share their supplier information with you. Be careful when approaching store owners so that they do not view you as competition. Your best bet is to visit stores outside of your geographic location and explain your situation. Put yourself on the other side. If you were the business owner and someone asked you where you got your items, would you want to help? You would probably be more likely to help if the person was friendly, honest, and told you they were from a town far away.

Entrepreneur Profile

Beth Thomas
Redwood Children's Center
Redwood City, CA

Child care has long been a popular option for stay-at-home moms who want to generate an income; however, this mom waited until her kids were grown to devote her life to taking care of children. Beth Thomas, 57, is the owner of Redwood Children's Center, a pre-school that serves 51 families and maintains a list of up to 70 families waiting for a chance to enroll.

Thomas was an active mom of two boys who supported her husband with his real estate business. Like more than 50% of Americans, Thomas's marriage ended in divorce—leaving her wondering what to do with the rest of her life. She decided to take classes in Early Childhood Education (ECE) and took a job at a preschool in 1992.

Five years later she formed a partnership with the owner of the school and together they opened a second school in Redwood City, CA in 1999. Personality conflicts and mounting stress prompted Thomas to dissolve the partnership three years later. "The desire to operate my own business was the motivating factor."

"My partner wanted me to be more of a manager, but I wanted to be in the school," says Thomas. "I have a passion for teaching and I love the every day interaction with the children and their families. That's what brings me joy."

Running a child care center means that Thomas has to meet a lot of government-imposed regulations. "It's difficult to find a building with the square footage that I need inside and out.

That's why so many centers are located in churches and schools because they're already set up to meet the requirements." Regulations require that the site has 35 square-feet of space per child inside, and 75 square-feet of space outside.

The Redwood Children's Center is licensed by the Department of Social Services (DSS). Inspectors from the DSS can drop in anytime without warning. "Whatever they ask for, you just have to hand over," says Thomas. That includes files on children and staff.

Teachers at the school must have ECE units, first aid, and CPR certification. The school must also maintain a ratio of one teacher to every twelve students. Staffing levels are critical and Thomas says, "Finding and keeping quality employees is by far my biggest challenge." She has tried a variety of methods to locate new employees and says that the ads she's placed on Craigslist.org have produced the best results.

"There is a balance between what you can charge working parents and what you can pay employees to keep them," says Thomas. She tries to be flexible with her employees, allowing them time out to attend to medical appointments and other personal errands. "By doing that, I'm hoping they will be less inclined to call in sick," a situation that means Thomas has to fill in for the missing teacher.

On a typical day, Thomas spends her time on paperwork, filling in for teachers who are out, and even deals with janitorial and plumbing mishaps. "I'm the typical small business owner. There is no job that I don't do because that's what it takes to make a business work."
The only advertising expense comes from an ad in the phone book since word of mouth keeps the waiting list filled with anxious families. "The need for quality childcare and preschools

is phenomenal," says Thomas. She doesn't see the potential implementation of universal childcare as a threat. "Parents have the right to choose. We do a better job so I don't worry about it affecting my business."

Because business is booming, Thomas says she would like to expand her center to serve 100 children and offer infant-care through kindergarten. Unfortunately, her business is located on the cusp of the Silicon Valley, an area where real estate prices run high. As she continues her search for a bigger and better location, she certainly seems to be enjoying the ride. "I enjoy being a mentor for my teachers and also with the parents. Educating the parents can be difficult because they are afraid to be parents and to say no. Children need boundaries."

As for her decision to run the business on her own, Thomas says, "I'm a committee of one. It's easier to make a decision. I can also decide to take next week off and don't have to worry about running it by someone else."

Though there are long hours and hiring challenges, Thomas says, "You have to be willing to take the downside along with the upside. In my case, the reward is so much bigger than the downside."

Thomas says that she wouldn't do anything differently. "I like to think that life has a plan. All those years of experience as an employee and a teacher prepared me for what I'm doing now. This isn't a field where you can read a book and go do it. You have to have lots of common sense."

Her advice for entrepreneurs: "It's not as scary as we immediately think it is. And if you do what you love, all of the other pieces fall into place."

Quick Tip

If you spend any amount of time on the phone, invest
in a headset. They are relatively inexpensive and allow
you to keep your hands free while talking so you can file
loose papers, take notes, or straighten up while talking.
A headset is also essential for anyone with a cell phone
in the car

Chapter 10

Business Tools & Essentials

*"Many of life's failures are people who did not realize how
close they were to success when they gave up."*
–Thomas A. Edison

Whether your office is home-based or at another location,
you will need to stock it with essential supplies while
sticking to your budget.

Office Furniture

While reducing costs is always important for a new business
owner, a comfortable and functional office is also important. If
you are going to spend a significant amount of time at your desk,
your best investment is in a quality chair.

An ergonomic chair can mean the difference between back pain
and fatigue, and a productive and comfortable environment. Test
drive chairs by visiting office supply and furniture stores. Many
chair manufacturers even list the recommended duration of use
for each chair. Some chairs are rated for casual use (up to three
hours per day) and others are rated for moderate and heavy use.
Often these chairs cannot be returned once purchased, so make
your decision carefully.

If you are going to spend any length of time at your desk, you
want to find one that suits your needs and gives you a productive
environment. A fancy desk is not necessary unless you are in
a business that needs to project a particular image to clients.
Used desks can be purchased at thrift stores, consignment stores,

through classified ads and garage sales. Inexpensive desks can be found in the large discount stores such as Target or Wal-Mart. IKEA (www.ikea.com) offers modular office furniture at reasonable prices that can outfit an entire office building.

The large office supply chains, such as Office Depot, Staples and Office Max, offer a great selection of desks in all price ranges. One advantage of shopping these stores online is that delivery is usually free, so you will avoid the hassle of transporting a large, bulky item yourself. Visit their websites and sign up for mailing lists to receive special discount offers and sale notices.

√ www.officedepot.com/
√ www.officemax.com/
√ www.staples.com/

Of course there are always high-end furniture companies and custom furniture outfitters that can meet the needs of a flashy new office for those lucky enough to have a large budget.

Computers

Though computer prices have come down over the years, these essential machines will still take a bite out of your budget. If you aren't computer savvy, be sure to get some expert advice by visiting a local electronics store so you can talk to someone in person. Performance should always be a consideration so look for models with faster processors and a lot of Random Access Memory (RAM). Disk space (hard drive) is important in allowing you to store as much data as possible, so a system with at least 20 gigabytes of hard drive space would be best.

You will also need a modem to access the Internet unless you choose to use a Digital Service Line (DSL). Many systems now include a CD burner which can come in handy for backing up large amounts of data, or saving data to send to advertisers, your accountant or for other business transactions.

The software you choose is also important. For a simple business, you will probably need a basic word processing program such as Microsoft Word, a spreadsheet program such as Excel and an accounting program such as Quicken or QuickBooks. Microsoft has several bundled packages to meet the needs of businesses so compare the offerings and the prices to determine what your business requires. Some other programs that you may want to consider are:

√ **Microsoft Publisher** - This is a handy program for designing your own fliers, brochures, postcards, and even business cards. Visit www.Microsoft.com.

√ **Microsoft FrontPage** or **Macromedia Dreamweaver** – These programs are used for website design. Visit www. Microsoft.com or www.Macromedia.com.

√ **Adobe Acrobat** - This program allows you to create PDF documents which compress the data and make documents easy to download to most computers. PDF documents are handy for large Word documents, scanned files, and any data that you want to distribute to the public. You can also create e-books in PDF format. Visit www.adobe.com.

About the only place computers aren't yet for sale is in grocery stores, so your options for purchasing are abundant. The choices can also be overwhelming for a novice computer user. If you don't have a lot of computer experience, enlist someone who does to help you with your buying decision. If you want some help from a knowledgeable sales person, visit an electronics store such as Best Buy, Circuit City or Fry's Electronics. The individual manufacturers also sell their own computers. Check out www.Dell.com, www.IBM.com or www.HP.com. Mac users can visit www.Apple.com.

If you plan to set up your own network or data center with servers and large computers, you may want to investigate your hardware decisions with the enterprise computer companies. Most of them offer small business price breaks on servers and equipment in hopes that your business grows and you will continue to invest with them. Both IBM and Sun Microsystems offer special pricing and even financing for small businesses.

The maintenance and protection of your computer is critical. The simplest way to protect your computer is with a surge protector that you can buy at the hardware store or office supply shop. A surge in power can fry your system, so a $15 surge protector is a wise investment. An Uninterrupted Power Supply (UPS), also known as a battery backup system, provides continuous power in the event of an outage. These come with various amounts of backup power—the smallest will keep your computer running for twenty minutes—allowing you time to save the programs you have open and shut your computer down safely. If your computer is critical to your business, you will probably want to invest in a UPS that stays on for a longer duration so business is not interrupted.

If your computer crashes, you risk losing all of your data if you don't have it backed up. Most PCs are preloaded with free backup software that you can configure to run at specified intervals. You can also invest in more comprehensive backup technologies from companies like Veritas (www.Veritas.com) or Computer Associates (www.ca.com). Many website hosting companies also offer online backup services. Don't risk your business and the loss of your data without backup protection.

Viruses are a rampant problem in the computer age, especially with PCs that access the Internet. You will need to purchase virus protection which usually involves an annual subscription fee of less than $30. The most common virus protection applications are offered by McAffe (www.McAfee.com) and Symantec (www.Symantec.com).

Printer

When shopping for a printer, first determine your needs and then compare your options. If you are going to need multiple printers, you will probably want to stick with similar models to simplify and save costs when ordering replacement ink and toner cartridges. Printers have become relatively inexpensive because the manufacturers make most of their money on the ink cartridges—an important factor to keep in mind when doing your research.

Sites such as www.BizRate.com, www.Buy.com and www. ePinions.com all offer comparison shopping services. These sites allow you to compare prices and read customer reviews for individual products. You can also visit office supply stores and read detailed information on printer cartridges, including the number of pages each will produce before it has to be replaced. Anticipate the volume of printing you will do and compare the prices of the appropriate cartridges to determine what makes the most financial sense.

Costco shoppers will find a reasonable assortment of printers available as well as an array of ink cartridges. It may be wise to consider printers that use cartridges you can purchase at Costco since their retail mark-up is significantly lower than most office supply houses.

There are many multi-function printers available now so decide what functions you need to run your business effectively. These "All-in-One" systems can be a great solution for a small business. Some of the features available are:

√ **Printing in color** (in addition to basic black and white) is handy for printing small quantities of fliers, business cards, reports, and brochures. While color cartridges are more expensive than their black ink counterparts, the value can be great when it comes to creating a professional image for your business. Color copies at copy centers can run as high as $1.00 each, so when you factor in the page counts that an ink cartridge should provide, you will find that the savings can be worth the investment.

√ A **scanner** can be useful for numerous functions. If you need to e-mail a copy of a document or picture to someone, you can use your scanner to create an image file and quickly send the copy off through e-mail. You can also scan photos that can be uploaded to your website or sent to the companies that you advertise with.

√ **Copies** can be generated on many multi-function printers. This feature is practically essential to any type of business. Whether you need to make a quick copy of an invoice or run off several copies of a flier, most machines can handle small jobs. If you anticipate a high volume of copies, then you are probably better off to purchase a copy machine or lease one from a major copy machine vendors (Xerox, Cannon, Sharp, Ricoh, etc.)

√ **Fax** capabilities can be useful depending on your need for this service. If you intend to receive a high volume of faxed documents, you may want to consider a separate fax machine or online fax service. If your fax needs are minimal to moderate, having them bundled with your printer could be useful. Keep in mind the location of your printer and that it will need to have access to a phone line to accept or send faxes.

√ Some printers can be **networked**, allowing multiple users to print from different computers on the same network. If your office has multiple computers, this can be a cost-saving option.

Fax

Depending on your anticipated usage for faxes, you should decide whether you need a dedicated fax machine or one that is bundled in with your printer. Another option is to use an online fax service.

A service like eFax (www.efax.com) lets you receive faxes for free via e-mail attachments. The company will even issue you your own phone number, though the free service does not allow you to specify an area code in your region so you will end up with a long distance number. For a nominal monthly fee, you can have a fax number assigned in your area code and receive faxes at no additional charge. There is a small per-page fee for sending faxes (currently around $.10 per page). Faxes can be sent from your computer using file attachments such as word processing documents or image files (that you scan in with a scanner). This is a useful service if your office is mobile, since you can send and receive faxes from any computer.

Phone Service

The phone company is surprisingly helpful when setting up a business line and will give you a variety of phone numbers to choose from. Be sure to figure out some letter combinations before you call to set up your business line.

For example, if you have a pet business, you might want to try to have a number like 555-PETS or 555-WOOF. If your combination is available with any of the prefixes for your area, you can get that number at no extra charge! Prefixes may also spell out catchy phrases or words. Be prepared before you call so you don't have to rush to make a decision

Postage and Shipping

If you are going to be shipping packages, you will want to be as self-sufficient as possible. Even if you only ship one or two packages each day, the time it takes to stand in line at the post office or mail center can really add up.

Printing your own postage can save you time and can easily be accomplished with a standard printer. Two of the most popular services are www.Stamps.com and www.Endicia.com. You can also purchase stamps online and use the U.S. Postal Service's online calculators to determine shipping costs at: www.USPS. gov. The Postal Service offers free boxes, tape, labels, and stickers if you use Priority Mail, which you can order from the website and have shipped to you free of charge.

Depending on the size and weight of items you ship, you will need to evaluate your best provider options. The major carriers will pick up packages for free. Check out Federal Express (www.FedEx.com) and United Parcel Service (www.UPS.com) to compare service offerings in your area.

Shipping supplies can be expensive if you purchase them from your local office supply store. If you can find a local vendor for these supplies in bulk, the savings can be great. You can also order online from www.PaperMart.com, www.uline.com, or even from www.eBay.com. Be sure to compare prices and shipping charges since large quantities of bubble mailers may not weigh much, but they are often shipped in boxes that are considered oversized. Depending on where you live, the shipping might cause the cost to skyrocket if your order has to travel across the country.

Office Supplies

You will likely have an ongoing need for various office supplies so you should get established early with a provider near you. Many of the large stores offer free delivery (a great time saver) and rewards programs with discounts or even cash back on your purchase. The three main providers are www.OfficeDepot.com, www.OfficeMax.com, and www.Staples.com.

The big warehouse stores offer many supplies at great prices. If you have a membership and time to shop at one of these super centers, you could save some money by picking up supplies yourself.

Fixtures

Office furniture and fixtures can eat up a large chunk of your startup budget if you're not careful. Be sure to compare prices on items before you buy, and take your time making these purchases. One great option is to find a used fixture or supply warehouse in your area. Check your phone book or ask local retailers for suggestions.

If you are unable to locate local resources, there are plenty of online resources to choose from. If you are a member of a trade association, you should check there first for trusted recommendations. One company that I have used with great success is www.ValuDisplay.com. This is another area where you may be able to find the items you need from eBay. Also, don't forget to check your local classified ads for businesses that are closing. Many business owners practically give away their equipment when the company shuts down.

Stationery

Your business cards are an important reflection of you and your company. Prices for business cards and the rest of the stationery family can range dramatically and warrant some comparison shopping. Be sure to order your cards early on so that you are able to hand them out to everyone you encounter. Local resources are always a good option if you can find the right pricing,

I use www.iPrint.com for business cards and rubber stamps. Their prices are reasonable and I have been consistently satisfied with the quality of their products. They also have a handy tool that lets you design your own business cards, using a template that you can modify to meet your needs. Another popular online printing provider is www.vistaprint.com.

Make sure your business stationery is consistent and reflects the image you want to portray to the world. You might want to order in small quantities at first, since you may find that you want to change the look or information on your stationery once your business is off and running.

There are plenty of Internet sites that offer free business cards, but be aware that they will print their own logo on your cards. This advertisement may not be the best way to reflect the professionalism of your business. It would probably make more sense to invest the $30+ for a quality box of cards.

If you're in a pinch, you can design business cards using Microsoft Publisher. The office supply stores sell sheets of perforated cards that you can print yourself. The quality of these cards has improved greatly over time so it's nearly impossible to tell when you hand out a homemade card. Though it will be cheaper to have large quantities of cards printed professionally, printing some of your own cards can come in handy while you wait for your order or while you are still deciding on a printing company.

Signage

If you have a commercial location, you will need signage for the front of the building. Your landlord may recommend local sources (and may also outline requirements in your lease so be sure to check what you are allowed to use). One option is Fast Signs (www.FastSigns.com), a franchise that serves signage needs in communities across the U.S.

Electric signs (the lettered signs you see in strip malls and shopping centers) can take several weeks or even months to be manufactured, so it's a good idea to order early. Many cities require a permit to operate an electric sign. Your sign provider will let you know if this is the case and will often handle the permit process for you. These signs can also cost thousands of dollars so be sure to factor the cost into your budget.

You may also need banners and other types of signs that a local provider will be happy to handle. Window painting can also be a relatively inexpensive way to add to the appeal of your business or advertise your services. Check the phone book for sign providers and get quotes and references from several sources.

Be sure to give careful consideration to the color and general design of any signs you use. Many businesses use red because it stands out, but if you are in a location where everything is red, you won't stand out. Yellow can be eye-catching amongst a sea of other colors. Do your best to differentiate your business within the limits of your lease agreement.

Entrepreneur Profile
Michael Brooks
MarketSpark Media
Boise, ID
www.smallbizgames.com and www.thirdmindusa.com

Michael Brooks has gone from working on the presidential campaign for Ronald Reagan to running two businesses that benefit small business owners—a move that happened when he fell in love with Boise, Idaho.

Brooks, 46, worked as a lobbyist in California for several years before being transferred to Idaho for a two-year assignment. When the assignment was over, he decided he wanted to stay. With the help of business partner Lisa Kimsey, Brooks launched his first business in 2003.

Third Mind USA helps business owners participate in mastermind groups, also known as peer learning or brainstorming groups. Six participants from non-competing businesses meet monthly via teleconference to strategize and set monthly business goals. The meetings are run by a facilitator and the members hold each other accountable for meeting their goals each month.

The second company that Brooks and Kimsey launched is Small Biz Games, an Olympics-style awards program that recognizes small and micro-small business owners (those with less than 10 employees). Entrants receive recognition and compete for a chance to win cash prizes.

Since Brooks came from the political arena, he had to rely on books and online resources to learn about starting and running a small business. "I wrote a modified strategic plan prior to starting the business," he says. "My plan was about five pages and included our mission statement (strategy) and a monthly tactical plan on how to implement that strategy.

"From that document, each month I created a separate 30-day plan with daily goals (things to do each day) that would move the business forward toward the mini-objective of the 30-day business plan. I still do this today. I often joke with people in talks and say 'forget your long-term goals, focus on daily goals and you will achieve your long-term goals a heck of a lot faster.'"

Brooks primarily relies upon online resources for marketing his businesses, including pay-per-click search engines, e-zine advertising, and writing articles for distribution. He says, "Writing articles in your area of expertise can be an excellent way to gain exposure and is usually free!"

Media exposure is another way Brooks gets the word out about his companies. He uses press kits, press releases, and interviews. "In my experience, most small and home businesses do not understand the value of free publicity or do not believe they can be successful in getting something written about them. Free publicity is not just for the big boys. Almost every small or home business has a story a journalist somewhere will be interested in."

Like many entrepreneurs, Brooks admits to working an average of 60 hours per week. He says, "I get to my home office between 7:30 and 8:00 a.m., answer e-mail, return phone calls, handle administrative tasks, website maintenance, and do a lot of research until about 10:00 a.m. The rest of the morning I devote to marketing tasks. Afternoons are spent working with clients and whatever else pops up. No two days are ever the same, which makes it exciting and challenging. I often return to my office around 10:00 p.m. and work for another two or three hours."

Learning from his mistakes has helped Brooks refine his business goals. "I quit my job first and then began to develop my business, which I would not recommend. It can put a lot of financial pressure on a person and their family if the loss of income has not been accounted for. Always count on it taking twice as long as you think to become profitable."

Online marketing is another area where Brooks admits making some expensive mistakes. He advises others to "research your target market carefully and then choose marketing vehicles that can be measured in terms of response."

To deal with challenges, Brooks says he follows the advice of famous motivational speaker, Tony Robbins. "Robbins suggests that you take a step back from whatever challenge you may be facing and ask one simple question—'What is good about this problem?'—and then take several minutes to brainstorm and write down everything you can possibly think of on why this challenge is a good problem to have."

Brooks recently put this advice to the test when a keynote speaker for the Small Biz Games awards conference fell through. "Rather than being devastated, I sat back and asked what good can come of this. I wrote down several things, but the one that stuck out was that we might get someone even better. I asked for suggestions from people I knew and our other judges and we did just that—we landed someone even better than our first choice!"

Balancing family life is a priority for Brooks. He spends time with his wife, Teresa, and two stepchildren in the evenings and on weekends. He also maintains a standing weekly date night with Teresa. The couple tries to schedule a long weekend getaway every six weeks or so. "When your business is based in your home, sometimes you just have to set limits because your office is always there and there is always something that needs to be done. "

Brooks cites his favorite business books as "Winning" by Jack Welsh, "Zero to Six Figures" by Jennifer Keenan Bonoff, and the "Guerrilla Marketing" series by Jay Conrad Levinson.

Multiple income streams are a factor in this business owner's success. He has co-authored two books that are due out in late 2005. The majority of the revenues are currently coming from the Third Mind USA business, but Brooks hopes that the newly launched Small Biz Games will produce more revenues than all other services combined.

Brooks offers his advice to aspiring business owners: "Big business and especially micro-small and home businesses must continue to reinvent themselves with new ideas. I highly recommend always being on the lookout for new products or services that fit in with your business mission or strategy. "

Quick Tip

Print out a list of the supplies you use most often and post it somewhere for easy access. As you run low on things like tape or envelopes, make a note on the list so you can easily reorder before you run out completely. If you have employees, have them mark the list as well. Always keep extra essentials on hand such as printer cartridges and paper.

Chapter 11

Operations

"A positive attitude may not solve all your problems, but it will annoy enough people to make it worth the effort."
—Herm Albright

It's a good idea to get a handle on your operations long before you even launch your business. Procedures will change as you face the reality of running your business on a daily basis, but having a plan from the beginning is sure to make your business run more smoothly.

Operations Manual

Creating a manual may seem like a lot of extra work, but it can serve as a valuable training tool for your employees. You should also find that you learn quite a bit about your business when you put your manual together, because it forces you to consider all aspects of your business operations. You may want to have an online version and a version that is printed and placed in a binder for easy access.

I have an operations manual for my bookstore that my employees use to reference procedures that they don't encounter on a daily basis, such as refunds and gift certificates. The manual empowers them to run the business when I'm not there, and saves me from receiving anxious phone calls. I update the manual regularly when policies are changed or added and look to my employees for input. It is an essential tool for keeping everyone informed and our operations consistent.

When writing your manual, you want to cover as much as possible while keeping the instructions simple. Think about a typical day and what needs to happen throughout the day. Start by outlining the tasks of a typical day. Write in a conversational style and explain procedures in a step-by-step format. Make sure all of the directions are clear and that it doesn't leave the reader confused or with unanswered questions. When you are finished, ask some employees to read it and give you feedback.

Here are some topics that you may want to cover in your operations manual:
√ Company Overview & History
√ Mission Statement
√ Opening Procedures
√ Closing Procedures
√ Cash Handling
√ Daily Tasks
√ Alarm System Operations
√ Safe Opening and Closing Procedures
√ Contact Numbers for Emergencies or Information
√ Employee Shift Coverage
√ Website Procedures
√ Customer Service Procedures
√ Sales Procedures
√ Sales Quotas
√ Commission Payments
√ Order Processing
√ Credit Card Processing
√ Refunds and Returns
√ Gift Certificates
√ Special Orders
√ Shipping & Receiving
√ Equipment Handling
√ Equipment Maintenance (replacing printer cartridges, receipt tape, etc.)

√ Security Procedures
√ Emergency Procedures
√ Product Pricing and Discounts
√ Other Miscellaneous Procedures and Anything Specific to the
   Way Your Business Operates

Employee Manual

Large corporations use employee manuals to both educate
employees about policies and protect themselves legally.
Whether or not you need an employee manual is your decision,
though it can be a great tool for keeping your policies consistent.
You should have a manual like this reviewed by a lawyer to
make sure it is compliant with local and federal laws. The
following is a sample outline that you can use as a guideline for
your manual:

1. Welcome & Introduction
2. Purpose of Handbook
3. Company Mission Statement
4. Company History
5. Employee Responsibilities & Code of Conduct
6. Discipline Procedures
7. Attendance and Punctuality
8. Time Cards
9. Work Hours, Breaks & Lunch Breaks
10. Overtime Policy
11. Payday
12. Payroll Deductions
13. Cash flow statementnce Reviews and Wage Increases
14. Promotions
15. Resignation and Termination
16. Telephone Usage
17. Benefits Overview
    a. Medical
    b. Dental

    c. Vision
    d. Employee Assistance Program
    e. Vacation
    f. Sick Time
    g. Tuition Reimbursement
    h. Life Insurance
    i. Disability Benefits
    j. Employee Discount
    k. Employee Referral Bonus
    l. Years of Service Awards

18. Leave of Absence
    a. Sick
    b. Family Leave
    c. Funeral
    d. Disability
    e. Jury Duty
    f. Military
    g. Maternity
    h. Unpaid Leave

19. Emergency Procedures
20. Summary and Acknowledgement

Hiring Employees

There are many rules and regulations to follow when it comes to hiring employees. The following are some key topics to be aware of as you navigate through this process, along with additional resources.

Employee vs. Independent Contractor

There are strict rules around who is considered an employee and who can be labeled an independent contractor. Employees have schedules set by an employer, contractors set their own hours. Employees are trained by an employer; contractors use their own methods for performing work. Contractors are hired to complete one specific job and there is no ongoing relationship. If you need further clarification and want to review the 20-factor checklist that the IRS uses to determine if someone is an employee or a contractor, visit: www.ftmn.com/Employee.html.

Employer Identification Number (EIN)

If you are going to have employees, you will need to apply for an EIN, also known as a federal tax identification number. Sole proprietors without employees can usually use their social security number, but if you incorporate or pay employees, you will need to apply for an EIN. Refer to the list of state resources chapter eight find requirements for where you live.

Locating Employees

Word of mouth is a great way to begin your search for employees. Your friends, business contacts or family may be able to recommend someone. If you have existing customers, they can also provide a potential source for dependable workers. Let everyone on your mailing list know that you are looking for help. You can also place a classified ad through your local newspaper or on www.Craigslist.org, an online classified ad system with an established presence in most major cities. Other popular online destinations for job seekers are www.Monster.com and http://hotjobs.yahoo.com/.

Interviewing

You may want to screen potential job candidates by phone before bringing them in for a formal interview. Develop a list of questions that you want to ask either on the phone or during an in-person interview. Make sure that all of your interview questions are job-related and avoid discrimination in any form.

For example, you cannot legally require an applicant to have a medical exam, however you can ask the candidate to perform an agility test (such as carrying a 25 lb. package across the room) if applicable.

Employees with Disabilities

You cannot ask a potential employee if they have a disability, but you can ask if they are able to perform a specific job function or tasks. The Work Opportunity Tax Credit (WOTC) provides tax incentives for employing workers with certain disabilities, such as those who have a mental or physical disability resulting in a hindrance to employment.

The WOTC also provides a tax credit for employers who hire certain targeted low-income groups, including vocational rehabilitation referrals, former AFDC recipients, veterans, ex-felons, food stamp recipients, summer youth employees, and SSI recipients. This program allows an employer to take a tax credit of up to 40 percent of the first $6,000, or up to $2,400, in wages paid during the first twelve months for each new hire. There are additional tax incentives available for money spent on making your business accessible to people with disabilities. For more information about these tax incentives, visit the Department of Labor website at www.dol.gov/odep/pubs/ek97/tax.htm.

For a complete guide to hiring people with disabilities, referral programs and compliance information, visit the Social Security website at www.socialsecurity.gov/work/Employers/employers.html.

Reference Checks

Previous employers are only required to provide the employee's date of hire, date of termination, and job detail. They are not allowed to discuss any additional details, unless the employee has signed a waiver and a "hold harmless" agreement as a condition for applying for the job.

You can call the applicant's personal references, though keep in mind that these are probably friends of the applicant so you aren't likely to get an objective opinion. The personal references can be enlightening if the applicant has kept in touch with former teachers, mentors or other influential individuals. Regardless, it is always a good idea to check references so you get a better understanding of the person you are about to hire.

Credit Checks

Some companies that deal with financial issues require a credit check for potential employees. You must have the applicant sign an agreement in order to perform a credit check

Background Checks
Some states allow employers to base their hiring decisions on whether an applicant has a criminal history. Check your state's requirements to find out what your legal rights are if you intend to perform a background check: www.BusinessInfoGuide.com/regional.htm.

Wages

The current federal minimum wage is $5.15 per hour. However, each state has different laws that define minimum wages and overtime pay. To locate the laws for your state, visit www.dol.gov/esa/minwage/america.htm.

Employment Taxes and Payroll

While payroll can be done by hand, most people prefer to use a program such as QuickBooks Payroll or to hire an accountant, bank or service to handle payroll. Taxes must be withheld from employee checks and paid either monthly or quarterly by the employer. Your local bank probably offers payroll services for a nominal fee, or your accountant or bookkeeper will offer this service. If you are worried about meeting all of the requirements and deadlines, this can be a worthy investment.

To access the IRS Employment Tax publications, visit www.irs. gov/businesses/small/article/0,,id=98868,00.html.

Additional Employment Compliance Resources

Depending on the type of business you are running, you may be required to display posters from the Department of Labor. For a list of requirements and access to posters, visit www.dol.gov/osbp/sbrefa/poster/matrix.htm.

To download the complete Employment Law Guide from the U.S. Department of Labor (DOL), visit www.dol.gov/asp/programs/guide.htm. The DOL also has a special division devoted to small business compliance. The Office of Small Business Programs can be reached directly at 1-888-9-SBREFA.

Security Measures

Security for your business may seem like a To Do list item that you can put off until later, but you may regret it if you wait too long to implement security practices. Too many people don't worry about security until something goes wrong, which can be a hard way to learn. Home businesses have far fewer concerns about security than owners of retail or office locations, so the following topics may not be relevant if you are working from home.

Alarm System

A basic security alarm system is essential for retail and office locations. There are a variety of options to choose from, including motion detectors, broken glass detectors, and sensors on doors and windows. Most motion detectors only detect movement of anything over 25 pounds, which can prevent false alarms from rodents, small animals, or other minor occurrences.

Unfortunately, motion detectors can also be tripped by pests that get too close to the sensor, causing false alarms. This may be unavoidable if the occasional spider makes its way into your location. Most police departments respond to two or three false alarm calls free of charge, but will bill you for excess calls, so make sure to keep pest problems under control. Alarm calls are also low-priority calls to the police, so depending on other events that are occurring at the time of your alarm signal, it may take awhile for the police to arrive.

One handy advantage of alarm systems is that you can set the door chime to signal when someone enters or leaves your location. Some companies also offer a panic button, which can notify the police department instantly when pressed. If this is an important feature for your business, inquire with the security companies in your area since not all companies offer panic button service.

Surveillance Cameras

There are a wide variety of camera solutions available ranging from $100 to thousands of dollars. Cameras can provide evidence in the event of a crime, not only helping you locate the criminal, but helping you get a conviction. If someone steals from you, even if you can identify the criminal, it will be your word against theirs if you don't have the event on film.

The mere presence of security cameras can also deter theft. Make sure you post signs around your facilities letting people know that they are under surveillance. This alone could potentially prevent a crime. You can also install realistic-looking fake cameras for the same effect. These can be purchased for $20 to $30 from eBay or retail supply stores like www.Valudisplay.com. You can also purchase mirrors that can be placed in the corners of the room or overhead, giving you the ability to monitor patrons and letting patrons know that they are being watched.

Cash Handling

If you use a cash register, be sure to keep it locked when you step away from the counter. Most cash registers are equipped with an emergency release lever underneath, allowing you to open the cash drawer without any noise. Unfortunately many criminals know this, and if you run a small shop and aren't always near your register, savvy criminals can take advantage of the situation. To protect your register, bolt it down to the counter and train your employees to keep it locked at all times.

Make a point of doing a cash drop at regular intervals throughout the day. You don't want to have hundreds of dollars sitting in your cash register—especially a cash drawer that can be seen by the public. You may help resist the temptation of a criminal by keeping your drawer looking fairly empty, while also minimizing the amount of money lost in the event that a robbery occurs.

Keep your cash in a safe after-hours. Safes can be purchased for as little as $200 from any office supply store or from the big discount stores including Target and Wal-Mart. Also, use care when coming or going with large amounts of cash. You don't want to make it obvious that you are carrying cash out of the building at 6 pm every night. If you use a cash bag, hide it in a brief case or other type of container. Criminals like predictability and could watch you or your employees for days or weeks until they learn the patterns of your cash-carrying ways.

Basic Crime Prevention

Greet everyone who enters your premises with a friendly "hello." Studies show that this alone can prevent theft since you let each person know that you are aware of their presence. Criminals often work in teams, so trust your instincts and keep a close eye on anyone who looks suspicious. One common trick is for a pair of robbers to enter a small store; while one distracts the cashier by asking for assistance, the other is busy shoplifting or ripping off the register.

In the event of an armed robbery, it is usually safest to just hand over the cash. Trying to be a hero could prove to be dangerous, so get them out of the building as quickly as possible and call the police. It would also be wise to discuss these security measures with your employees and detail your policies in your operations manual.

Entrepreneur Profile

Tina Brooks and Greg Brooks
Peppermaster® Rigaud,
Quebec, Canada
www.peppermaster.com

Husband and wife team Greg and Tina Brooks combined their individual skills to build a hot company—literally. Peppermaster offers hot sauces and pepper-based products, and the company's success has transformed the lives of these savvy entrepreneurs.

Tina spent 20 years as a financial advisor and a self-described guerrilla marketer, while Greg spent 30 years as a chef and successful restaurateur. Greg also grew up in the Bahamas where he picked peppers off the limbs of bushes and developed a taste for the hottest and freshest peppers he could find. Together they decided to take their passion for hot peppers and an initial investment of just $250 to launch the company.

"The first thing we did was write a business plan," says Tina. "The plan was based on everything my husband knew about the specialty foods industry. We updated the information with intense research into the niche we wanted to target. Then it was full speed ahead."

They started by selling their sauces at the local farmers market and stuck closely to the details in their business plan. After just six months, they were achieving "exceptional success" and agreed to bring on another business partner—a decision they would soon regret.

Tina says that it wasn't long before the partner took complete control of the company and forced the couple to seek the counsel of a lawyer who advised them to "move on." She said, "We had a fantastic idea for a business that we knew would be intensely successful, but no money to run with it." Then disaster struck.

"When we got home, we discovered that the universe had different plans for us because our house was burning to the ground. So in the midst of trying to start a new business, we had to deal with losing our home and all our worldly possessions."

What started as a tragic event, Tina says, "turned out to have been a storm cloud with a silver lining." The insurance money from the house became seed money for the business. "We had to buy a new place to live so instead of buying a new farmhouse, we bought the town bakery."

The couple moved with their four children into the small apartment above the bakery and began transforming the building into workable space. "The kitchen where the sauces were manufactured had to be of a certain level of quality and it wasn't when we bought the building, but we sealed off parts of the kitchen with food grade plastic and did bits and pieces of the kitchen as we could afford to."

They built an office and a showroom, borrowing a desk from friends and furnishing their board room with patio furniture purchased at an end-of-season sale with a department store credit card.

Since the inception of their business in April 2004, Peppermaster boasts an offering of 24 different sauces, five of which generate the bulk of the revenue. Tina says, "I'm a marketing specialist, so I personally believe that our revenue comes from sales. And our sales come from marketing and marketing involves simply putting tastes on people's tongues. So the more people I can get to taste our product, the more people I can get to buy our product."

Tina admits that her husband has a different perspective. "He says that before you have sales, you have to have investment and that the appropriate timing of the investment spurs growth. So I guess you could say that what generates our revenues is our time and our money, our assets and commitment. These are the variables that your business plan clarifies. If you don't know what you have or how you can get there, you'll be spinning your wheels and fail to succeed."

Getting the word out about Peppermaster is one of Tina's primary tasks. She says, "Marketing isn't something you can do once and forget about; it's got to be continual, in your face. If anybody out there hasn't heard of you, then you have to tell them about yourself. They need to know who you are and why you are special."

Though she likes to work from nine to five, Tina says it doesn't always work out that way. "Sometimes you have to put in extra hours and if you aren't willing to do that, you won't succeed." She also strives to make work fit into her personal life, rather than the other way around. "We have things that we have to do that are more important than work and if I have to work when it's time to spend time with family, well, I bring the work to them." She uses a laptop and often works from her living room while simultaneously interacting with her children.

The road to sauce sales has been paved with challenges. Tina admits that they have made some mistakes along the way. Her biggest regret was not setting up their bookkeeping processes from day one. It took three months to repair the accounting problems and get the record keeping back on track.

She believes that the keys to their success are "a great concept, an astoundingly exceptional product, and an insatiable desire to introduce people to it."

For those considering a business partnership, Tina suggests drafting an "iron-clad partnership agreement." She adds, "I highly recommend a shotgun separation clause to save a lot of grief and anxiety in the event of discord."

Business books have been useful for the couple, but Tina cautions, "One individual book isn't the be-all and end-all of its information. It is important to use books as the tool to help gather information that you need to help move your business forward." She recommends "Business Plans for Dummies", or something like it, since she credits so much of her business success to her own business plan. She also likes university-level marketing books (text books). "You can kill this bird by taking a series of marketing courses at the local university, but I doubt most entrepreneurs have the time to do that."

She recommends that entrepreneurs attend industry-related trade shows, "even if you can't afford to be there." Since networking is an important factor in business success, Tina is a member of a number of organizations, including her local chamber of commerce and the International Virtual Women's Chamber of Commerce (www.ivwcc.org).

Tina would like to ultimately open a sales office in Nassau, Bahamas and intends to work toward her retirement goals. "We rework the business plan every few months so it's always on track. Ultimately our goal is to be financially independent on the beach. Following the business plan religiously is what is going to get us there."

Tina never let her fears get in the way of her dreams, and her passion for what she and her husband are doing is apparent. She says, "I was seriously afraid that we were the only ones that saw the opportunity and that even with all of our test marketing and industry study, we were wrong and we'd fall flat on our face. I'm pleasantly surprised every time my bank balance goes up."

Her final wisdom for aspiring entrepreneurs is something she seems to have mastered herself. "Dream it, want it, make it happen." She adds, "Surround yourself with people who are supportive of your vision. And if you don't have a vision, get one! You'll need it."

Chapter 12

The Business Plan

"There is no security on this earth, there is only opportunity."
–General Douglas MacArthur

You will need a business plan to obtain a small business loan. But even if you aren't seeking funding assistance, a business plan is an excellent tool for putting your business on the path to success. Writing a business plan forces you to think about all aspects of your business. Your plan should describe your business in great detail and though you may not have all of the answers yet, this is an excellent exercise to help you identify what weaknesses exist in your plan so you can address them early on.

The following outline was provided by John Troland, owner of The Business Plan Group: www.businessbeatlive.com/business_ plan_group.htm. Troland has been a business consultant and developer of business plans for 39 years.

I. Company Description / Overview
  A. Nature of Business
    1. Individuals being served / their needs
    2. Why your area?
  B. Your Distinctive Competencies (primary factors that will lead to your success)
    1. Superior customer need satisfaction
    2. Production/service delivery efficiencies
    3. Personnel
    4. Geographic location

II. Market Analysis
  A. Target Markets
    1. Demographics
    2. Geographic location
    3. Seasonal/cyclical trends
  B. Competition
    1. Identification
    2. Strengths (competitive advantages)
    3. Weaknesses (competitive disadvantages)

III. Products and Services
  A. Detailed Product/Service Description (from the user's perspective)
    1. Specific benefits of product/service
    2. Ability to meet needs
    3. Competitive advantages

IV. Marketing and Sales Activities
  A. Overall Market Strategy
    1. Market penetration strategy
    a.Intended means (including advertising, promotion, printed matter, etc.)
    2. Growth Strategy

V. Management and Ownership
  A. Management Staff Structure
  B. Key Managers (including self)
    1. Name
    2. Position
    3. Primary responsibilities and authority
    4. Primary responsibilities and authority with previous employers
    5.Unique skills and experiences that add to your company's distinctive competencies
  C. Legal Structure of the Business

VI. Organization and Personnel
  A. Recruitment procedures
  B.S taffing levels

Additional Resources

For business plan resources and examples, visit: www. BusinessInfoGuide.com/bplans.htm.

You can purchase software to help you write your business plan. The software should be available through any office supply or electronics store. Here are some options:
√ Palo Alto Business Plan Pro
√ Business Plan Writer Deluxe
√ Business Plan Maker Professional

Financial Projections

In addition to your written business plan, you should also create financial projections. A cash flow forecast is an itemized list of your business expenses, revenue streams, and your net profit or loss. Creating projections can be frustrating since you can't really know for sure what kind of revenues to expect from a new business, but you have to do your best to estimate the performance of your business. This is where a trade association can also come in handy. Yours may be able to provide you with industry trends and estimates of how quickly you can expect your business to grow.

Without financial projections, you lack actual target numbers and control over your operating expenses. Like the business plan itself, even if you don't plan to use this document to get a loan, developing a cash flow statement will be a valuable exercise in understanding the financial outlook for your business.

The following is an example of a simplified cash flow projection for Carly's Cookie Shop:

Cash Flow Forecast - Year 1 - Carly's Cookie Shop			
Description	January	February	March
Revenue			
In-store Sales	$2,500	$3,200	$3,600
Internet Sales	$480	$670	$740
Total Revenue (cash in)	$2,980	$3,870	$4,340
Cost of Goods (cash out)			
Ingredients	$480	$620	$700
Product Packaging	$110	$130	$150
Total Cost of Goods	$590	$750	$850
Expenses (cash out)			
Accounting Fees	$100	$100	$100
Advertising	$250	$250	$250
Baking Supplies	$80	$0	$20
Bank Fees	$20	$20	$20
Insurance	$150	$150	$150
Loan Interest	$150	$150	$150
Misc. Supplies	$420	$280	$150
Office Supplies	$70	$60	$30
Owner Draw	$0	$0	$0
Payroll	$600	$700	$700
Postage & Delivery	$60	$70	$90
Rent	$1,100	$1,100	$1,100
Security	$30	$30	$30
Telephone	$80	$90	$90
Utilities	$240	$250	$250
Total Expenses	$3,350	$3,250	$3,130
Final Calculations:			
Opening Balance (cash)	$12,000	$12,000	$12,000
Plus Revenues	$2,980	$3,870	$4,340
Less Cost of Goods	$590	$750	$850
Less Expenses	$3,350	$3,250	$3,130
Ending Balance	$11,040	$11,870	$12,360
Revenues	$2,980	$3,870	$4,340
Less Cost of Goods	$590	$750	$850
Less Expenses	$3,350	$3,250	$3,130
Net Income or Loss:	-$960	-$130	$360

Try This:

Use an Excel spreadsheet to create your own cash flow projection. Create a separate page or worksheet for each of the first three years of business. List the twelve months of the year across the top row of each page, and your itemized details down the left column. Make sure to include subtotals and calculations at the bottom of the page.

Here is an explanation of the items to list down the left side of your spreadsheet:

Revenue

List line items for each product line or revenue stream for your business. Using a bookstore as an example, the revenue streams would be retail book sales, audio book rentals, online book sales, gifts, greeting cards, and wholesale book lots to vendors.

Cost of Goods

Here you will indicate your monthly costs of acquiring the goods for sale. Be sure to include the cost of any professional services that you use in order to create or implement your product.

Expenses

This will be a fairly long list because this is where you list all of your business expenses. Here are items you should include when applicable:
√ Advertising & Promotion
√ Automotive Expenses (if you are leasing a business vehicle)
√ Auto – Gas & Repairs (if you are leasing a business vehicle)
√ Bank Fees
√ Building Improvements

√ Commissions Paid Out
√ Computer Repair or Maintenance
√ Deposits on Property (probably a one-time fee listed with your startup expenses)
√ Dues and Subscriptions (for professional organizations or trade publications)
√ Equipment (copiers, fax machines, etc.)
√ Insurance – Liability
√ Insurance – Medical
√ Insurance – Officer's
√ Insurance – Worker's Compensation
√ Interest Payments
√ Garbage Disposal
√ Licenses & Fees
√ Meals & Entertainment
√ Office Supplies
√ Officer's Salary
√ Outsourced Services (janitorial, plant care, window cleaning, etc.)
√ Postage & Shipping
√ Professional Fees – Accounting
√ Professional Fees – Legal
√ Rent for Premises
√ Rent for Equipment
√ Security
√ Supplies – General (paper cups, towels, cleaning products, etc.)
√ Telephone – Main
√ Telephone – Cell
√ Telephone – Internet or DSL Service
√ Travel
√ Utilities – Electric
√ Utilities – Gas
√ Utilities – Water

Employee Labor

If you have employees, here you will list the expenses for each group of employees such as general staff, management or contractors. You should also list payroll taxes as an expense, a 401K plan if you offer it, and any other contributions that you make to employee benefits.

Finishing and Evaluating the Cash Flow Projection

Tally up your expenses at the bottom and subtract them from the projected revenues. This gives you your overall profit or loss projection. Remember that most businesses take months or even years to reach the profitable stage. However, if your cash flow projections don't reflect profitability in a reasonable amount of time, this is the time to reevaluate your revenue streams and expenses. Can you increase sales for a product line? Add a new product line? Reduce expenses by limiting your payroll or rent expenses?

This is where the real value of this projection comes in. Now is your chance to see how viable your business model will be. You don't want to start a business without some evidence that you can make a profit. Evaluate your strategy carefully and make adjustments as needed.

Entrepreneur Profile

Lynda Gene Lippin
balanCenter Pilates
Narberth, PA
www.balancenter.com

Lynda Gene Lippin has learned how to overcome obstacles and run a successful business, despite two failed business partnerships. One led to a legal battle over a non-compete contract, and the other drove her into bankruptcy. Some people might give up, but these experiences only fueled this entrepreneur's desire to succeed.

Lippin and her husband, Tony L. Pitts, are the owners of balanCenter Pilates, a studio located in a busy office building in Pennsylvania. Lippin discovered her passion for Pilates while working on her philosophy degree at Purchase College. During grad school, she responded to an ad for a Pilates instructor, and has been in love with the method ever since.

To write her business plan, Lippin relied on a copy of "The Complete Idiot's Guide Business Plans" and opened her studio in 1998. "Everything and nothing prepared me for opening my own business," says Lippin. "I'm not sure why I wanted to open my own business, but I did always think that if I had to bust my ass, it might as well be for myself!"

BalanCenter offers up a host of services including individual instruction, group classes, Pilates certification for instructors, and special events. The instructors also work with clients who are living with physical conditions like fibromyalgia (a disease that causes chronic muscle pain), multiple sclerosis, osteoporosis, and arthritis.

Training session fees are based on the instructor's level of expertise. A private session with an Apprentice-level instructor is $35 and a session with a Master instructor costs $80.

To get the word out about her business, Lippin says, "We have mostly marketed through word of mouth," and adds that she also advertises with direct mail coupon ads. Some of her clients work for local news stations and have helped her get air time on newscasts. Lippin also writes a column for PhillyFIT magazine— an excellent opportunity to give her and her business credibility and exposure in the community.

Her passion for staying on top of the latest in Pilates practice keeps her at the top of her game. She says, "Over the years I have taken lots of seminars in Pilates, exercise science, anatomy, etc. I now have many certifications and am still hungry for more knowledge. I find the body and its systems to be fascinating and I'm always learning as much as I can."

An average work week for Lippin is about 60 hours. "In a typical day I see my first client at 8 a.m. and my last client at 7 p.m. When I do a training weekend, I am teaching a group of six to twelve teachers from 9 a.m. to 6 p.m. each day."

Clients are the primary focus at balanCenter. According to Lippin, "We strive as a company to serve our clients with care and respect; to always put them first and do our best to create good exercise programs and experiences for them so they stay healthy and happy." She also says that many of her clients are savvy business people who have served as mentors for her business practices.

Overcoming obstacles seems to have made this entrepreneur stronger. "I've had many challenges, legal, financial and health-wise," says Lippin. "At one point I bounced payroll and paid my staff in cash every week! But in the end, I'm still here, the studio's doing well, all my staff is still with me, so things could be much worse."

Lippin plans to expand her current location when the space next door becomes available. She is also working on a book proposal and wants to travel and teach Pilates in regions around the world.

Her advice for new entrepreneurs is to, "love what you do, because you will be doing a lot of it. And try to have enough money set aside, just in case." She adds, "You will work your ass off and it will take years to really see the result, but when you start to see glimmers of success, you will be so proud of yourself—and that's the best thing about owning your own business!"

Chapter 13

Marketing Plan

"Many a small thing has been made large
by the right kind of advertising."
–Mark Twain

A marketing plan should be part of your business plan, but it is so important that it deserves its own line item on your checklist. Marketing is what you do to let people know about your business and attract clients. It is critical to your business to have a plan to reach your customers. Unfortunately, you can't just flip on the Open sign and expect people to show up.

Marketing is not just another expense like a utility bill or office supplies. When done correctly, marketing is an investment in your business. Spending money on marketing should ultimately deliver a return on your investment and then some (an increase in profits). The money spent on marketing only feels like an expense when the program isn't working. As a new business owner, you will face some trial and error as you test different marketing options and determine which strategies work best for you. *You should plan to invest heavily on marketing in the first six months to two years to get your business off to the right start.*

Determining how to reach your customers is one of the biggest challenges you will face with your marketing strategy. Start by examining where your competitors advertise. Follow their lead since they have probably already figured out what venues works best. But they may not yet have tapped into all of the right sources for advertising; therefore, you should do some research and test out other opportunities.

Marketing is a combination of advertising and publicity. Advertising is something you typically pay for, like an ad in the newspaper. Publicity brings attention to your business through articles about your business in the media or when you host activities such as contests. Not all of your marketing has to be expensive. There are many ways to obtain free and low-cost publicity.

Press Releases

One of the most effective methods for promotion is media exposure—exposure that starts from a simple press release. Newspapers, magazines, radio, and television news shows rely on press releases to locate news and human interest stories. When your company is mentioned in a news article, it not only brings attention to your business, but it can add credibility to your business. The first major story that ran in the newspaper about my bookstore caused my sales to double that month, and increased my overall revenues in the months that followed.

Anyone can send a press release, but in order to get the attention of reporters, it must be professional, news-worthy and appealing to a broad audience.

A press release should be brief. One page is best, and two pages is a maximum. The release should include enough details so that a reporter could write a short article based solely on the information provided. The release should not be an announcement that a business or product simply exists, but should have an enticing "hook". Good hooks include special events (like a grand opening or anniversary), product announcements, contests, survey results or awards given or received. The trick is to make the hook interesting enough to capture the attention of the reader.

Be careful with your wording to avoid sounding like a sales brochure—this is sure to discourage the media from pursuing the story. Read several sample press releases before writing yours so you understand the proper format. Some good sources for reading professional releases are www.BusinessWire.com and www.PRNewswire.com. Follow these rules to write a press release that gets the attention you want:

√ Start with a proper heading that includes your contact information. When listing phone numbers, indicate a day and evening number (reporters may call at odd hours) or simply list your cell phone number.

√ Give the release an enticing title that captures the reader's interest and print it in **bold type**.

√ Double space the body of your release for easy reading.

√ The first paragraph should include the basics of who, what, where, when and why. You want to lay the foundation and include your hook immediately. Remember that you want to capture the attention of the media and get them excited about your story.

√ Determine the purpose of your press release. Is it to announce a grand opening, special event, introduce a new product or share valuable information with the public? Include the key points that make your story interesting.

√ Use quotes from business partners, clients or other professionals to give the story more color and credibility. As awkward as it may be, you may want to quote yourself— especially if you are the subject of the release.

√ Close with a brief summary of the business or the person you are promoting.

√ Do not allow grammar or spelling mistakes to sneak into a press release. Make sure you edit your writing thoroughly and have a friend—or better yet, two friends—review it for errors and content.

You should start by sending your press release out locally, even if you are aiming for a national audience. Local media is always a great place to start since you are part of the community.

Start compiling a list of media contacts. Check the websites of your local newspapers, news programs and magazines for contact names and address information. Media outlets accept press releases by mail, fax or e-mail and typically indicate their preferences on the website or publication masthead. If you can't locate press release instructions, it is best to mail it directly to the appropriate editor for your topic.

You can expand your reach and send your release directly to big publications nationwide. It will take awhile to compile a contact list so start early. You can also purchase a media list from a PR firm like Gebbie Press (www.gebbiepress.com), but be prepared to spend some cash since lists start around $140. Gebbie Press also offers a directory of websites for locating print, television, and radio station websites that you can access for free.

There are numerous services that you can pay to distribute your release to hundreds or thousands of markets. A few to in-vestigate are www.ereleases.com, www.prweb.com, and www.xpresspress.com. Some sites offer to send free press releases, and others promise more exposure the more you spend. I have heard from several people who said they were interviewed by reporters after sending press releases at the $30 level through PRWeb, though not everyone is as lucky.

Before you send your release, be sure you are prepared to answer interview questions. You may receive calls from reporters immediately and will want to have thoughtful responses ready. Consider writing a list of points you want to make and keep it handy.

Most people find that a press release can be worth its weight in gold since a news story usually generates more buzz than any form of paid advertising. Don't be discouraged if your first attempt doesn't receive the attention you want; simply try again until you find the formula and pitch that works.

I submitted the following release through PRWeb.com and received tremendous response and website traffic as a result:

Press Release

BusinessInfoGuide.com
5800 Madison Ave., Suite W, Sacramento, CA 95841
Contact: Stephanie Chandler, Owner
E-mail: **Stephanie@BusinessInfoGuide.com**

NEW WEBSITE FOR ENTREPRENEURS FINDS ITS NICHE BY PROVIDING LINKS TO INDUSTRY INFORMATION

January 20, 2005 – Sacramento, CA - BusinessInfoGuide.com went live on January 10th and acts as a directory for entrepreneurs by offering links to trade associations and publications, products, articles and other resources needed to start and run a business. The directory currently offers information for starting the following types of businesses: antiques & collectibles, cleaning (home & commercial), eBay, food & beverage, gift baskets, health & fitness, Internet & computers, pet services, public speaking, publishing, sports, travel, and a variety of retail businesses.

Owner Stephanie Chandler says she was frustrated when researching how to open a bookstore in 2003. "The Internet is full of how-to advice, but I had a hard time locating information specific to my industry. I needed to find trade associations and learn about book collecting and book selling, and it took countless hours of Internet surfing to find what I needed."

After fleeing an 11-year career in the Silicon Valley in 2003, Chandler opened Book Lovers Bookstore in Sacramento and began considering the need for BusinessInfoGuide.com. She says, "I began networking with other business owners and realized that they had the same problems I had. After a friend opened a retail store in San Francisco, I asked him what the most daunting part of the process was. He said, 'finding my vendors and trade associations.' The minute he said it, I knew I was onto something."

The site lists books specific to each industry and provides links directly to Amazon.com. There are also links to business licensing requirements for each of the fifty states, and a variety of vendors are already listed on the site making it easy for prospective entrepreneurs to get started.

Chandler is adding new information daily and promises more industry guides, vendor links, and articles are on the way. She already boasts steady site traffic and subscription requests for her free business newsletter. She adds, "We're in a time when job satisfaction is low and more and more people are considering starting their own businesses. It shouldn't be that difficult to find what you need and get started. For me, leaving corporate America was the best decision I've ever made. I want to help other people find the same happiness."

*BusinessInfoGuide.com provides resources and industry information for entrepreneurs. For more information, visit **www. BusinessInfoGuide.com.***

Distribute Fliers

Depending on the size and scope of your business, you can distribute fliers door to door in your neighborhood or hire some kids to do it for you. Fliers can also be left on the windshields of cars in busy parking lots or on the counters of other businesses. Simply ask the owner if you can leave your fliers or business cards and offer to return the favor at your location.

One local Realtor canvassed my neighborhood just before Memorial Day. She stuck an inexpensive American flag in the lawn in front of every single house, and then left her business card on each door step. This was an impressive way to get the attention of an entire neighborhood. The effort left us feeling a bit more patriotic as we drove through the neighborhood and admired all the flags waving in the wind. If this Realtor was really savvy, she could do it again for Independence Day, Veteran's Day, and all of the other patriotic holidays and brand herself as "the flag lady."

Create a Promotion, Contest or Giveaway

Brainstorm ideas for a contest with clearly defined rules and an attractive reward. Pay attention to how other businesses are running these types of promotions. Many restaurants have a jar to drop in your business card for a weekly drawing to receive a free lunch. This is an excellent way to build up a newsletter database since you will gather cards with e-mail and mailing addresses. You could also hold a coloring contest for kids, let the local schools know, and offer awards to the top entries.

One Northern California restaurant announced a "Bald Tuesday" promotion where balding individuals eat free on Tuesdays. Sound ridiculous? The media loved it. The restaurant was featured on the local news programs and eventually even received national attention.

Off-the-wall promotions can be some of the most effective, just be careful not to violate any laws. For example, one California business got in trouble for offering a free product to patrons wearing an "I Voted Today" sticker following the last presidential election.

Offering a free giveaway item is an excellent way to attract customers. You could offer something free with purchase, like a menu item or an inexpensive product. Special reports or tips booklets are relatively easy to create and distribute. If you owned a pet-related business, you could hand out tips on keeping pets healthy. If you owned an accounting firm, you could hand out tax planning advice with little-known loopholes to save people money.

Examine what other businesses in your area are offering their customers to get ideas. Some restaurants offer a free entrée or dessert with purchase. I've held special offers at my bookstore where kids get to pick out a book for free. Use your imagination and create something fun that the public will respond to. Don't forget to send a press release announcing the promotion.

Yellow Pages Ad

Ads in the phone book are expensive but crucial for many kinds of businesses. Internet companies are the exception since to advertise in the yellow pages across the world would cost more than even Donald Trump could afford. If you want to be listed in the yellow pages, be sure to get your ad in early since the phone book only comes out once each year and you don't want to miss the deadline. You may also have to place ads in several books, since most areas have more than one company that distributes phone books.

When deciding on your advertising strategy, evaluate the ads that comparable businesses are running. How can you compete with them? Just because an ad is bigger does not mean it is the most effective. Study ads throughout the phone book and decide which ones you like best.

Take your time when working with your yellow pages ad representative to find out what the best package offering is for your business. The phone company releases new packages and programs each year, and it is not easy to sift through all of the offerings (which they probably won't send you in print form, so you will have to rely on a sales person to explain your options). Take notes when talking to your sales representative and ask her to show you examples of what your money can buy.

Discuss advertising in multiple cities if it makes sense for your business. If you're in a small town, you may want to run ads in neighboring cities or in the phone book for the nearest big city. Most yellow pages companies offer discounts for multiple listings.

Create a Customer Database

Repeat business should account for a significant portion of your revenues, so marketing to your existing customers should be a constant priority. After only six months, the owners of De La Sole Footwear in San Francisco had amassed a customer database of over 1000 people because they asked every customer at the time of purchase if they would like to be added to the mailing list—a wise strategy.

Start generating your customer database from day one. You could ask your customers to sign up for your mailing list or gather their contact information through a jar where they drop their business cards. Make sure to post a privacy notice and assure them that you will never share their contact information with anyone—and keep your promise.

Send a Newsletter

A newsletter is an opportunity to create ongoing communications with your customers and to advertise new products, services or events. Give readers a reason to read and keep your newsletter by including a special coupon, recipe or useful article. You may want to expand your newsletter by selling or trading advertising space with other businesses. Here are some topic ideas for inclusion in your newsletter:

√ Brief letter to your customers
√ Calendar of events
√ New product announcement
√ Promotion or sale information
√ A coupon
√ A recipe
√ A handy idea or tip
√ Highlight a product
√ Explain the advantages of a product
√ Quotes from satisfied customers
√ Case studies
√ Advertisements for other businesses
√ Community information

Sending newsletters through e-mail is virtually free. In most cases, the biggest investment will be in your time. An e-mail newsletter does not need to be flashy. It's more important that it is easy to read. Using graphics can make it difficult for some customers to open or even receive your message, so minimize or eliminate the use of graphic images.

If you don't want to write all of the content yourself, you can access free articles on a variety of topics from websites like www.IdeaMarketers.com, www.ezinearticles.com, and www. Amazines.com. You could also have your employees or even your customers contribute some of the content. Don't forget to include your business contact information, hours of operation, and website URL in all of your correspondence with customers.

Microsoft Publisher has templates for print newsletters that are user friendly and allow you to create attractive and professional publications. You can have your newsletter printed at your local copy shop. Color copies are expensive, but may be worth the expense if you want to create a special image for your business. For a lower cost option, print your newsletter in black ink on pastel paper. You may also be able to qualify for bulk mail rates from the post office (www.usps.com).

Become an Expert in Your Field and Get Published

There are hundreds of ways to establish yourself as an expert. One inexpensive place to start is to volunteer for www.AllExperts. com. This website lists hundreds of subjects from sports and arts to business and automotive, and allows site visitors to ask questions of its volunteers. You can define how many questions you are willing to answer in a given day. This service allows you to gain exposure all over the world.

If you are skilled with the written word, offer to write articles for publications in exchange for promotion of your service, product or website. Trade magazines are an excellent place to start since they are often in need of writers. Consumer magazines can also be a source for your articles, although be aware that the popular magazines that you find on the checkout stands of grocery stores are the most difficult to break in to. It is best to start with smaller or regional publications.

For example, a career coach could write articles about job hunting, effective interview skills, negotiating salaries, and dressing for success. Study magazine articles and learn how to craft an article with a flair that fits the publication you are targeting. Once you have an effective story ready, write a short author biography and send it to an editor.

Locate magazines that you believe your article will appeal to and find the contact information for the editor. One great source for editorial contacts is an annual book called "Writer's Market" by Kathryn S. Brogan and Robert Lee Brewer. This hefty volume lists hundreds of publications, their rules for submission, and who to contact.

There is a protocol to follow when contacting magazine editors. Editors expect to be approached with a query letter. Use the following rules to write your query:

√ Use letterhead if you have it.

√ Make sure it is a professional business letter and include your contact information.

√ Address the letter to a specific person. Avoid "Dear Editor" as most find it offensive.

√ Open with a description of the subject and explain why it is important. Be concise and give enough detail to make it convincing, without being too wordy.

√ Explain your credentials.

√ Close with a polite salutation.

√ Most queries should be kept to one page.

√ If you have written articles for other publications, include 2 or 3 photocopies with your submission. In the publishing world, these are called "clips".

Here is a sample letter:

Dear Ms. Jones,

When job hunting, many women need help with writing an effective resume. There are key elements in writing a resume that many forget to employ. A resume should be:

♦ *Chronological.*

♦ *Written without spelling or punctuation errors.*

♦ *Tailored to the position for which the person is applying.*
♦ *Proofread by several people.*

I am a professional career coach and I have written a 1000-word article called "Resumes that Rock" that I am sending for your consideration. I hope you will agree that the readers of Women in the Workforce magazine will find this article useful.

Thank you for your time. I look forward to hearing from you.

Best regards,
Edna Entrepreneur

Send copies of two or three previously published articles if you have them. Also, add a short author bio at the end of the article you are submitting. Most magazines that offer a byline will allow only one or two sentences about the author. Your bio should look something like this:

"Edna Entrepreneur is a career coach in Dayton, Ohio. Visit her website at www.xxxxx.com."

Don't overlook websites that also accept article submissions. Many websites operate on a limited budget and appreciate articles written by experts. There are also several free content sites that allow you to post articles that others can reprint in their newsletters or e-zines. Check out the following websites:
√ www.ideamarketers.com
√ www.ezinearticles.com
√ www.articlecity.com
√ www.amazines.com

Additional Resources

If you are interested in learning more about freelance writing, visit these websites:
√ www.writersdigest.com
√ www.fundsforwriters.com
√ www.writersweekly.com
√ www.businessinfoguide.com/freelance.htm

Offer Referral Discounts

Many businesses offer a discount for referrals. One California hair salon sends a thank you card to anyone who refers a friend to them and includes a gift certificate for a future visit. This is an excellent way to build customer loyalty while attracting new clients. Create your own program and give your existing customers an incentive to send new business your way. Let your customers know that you appreciate it when they share your services with the people they know.

Host Events

If you have a location that can accommodate events, start booking them. Bookstores host author signings, financial firms offer financial presentations, restaurants offer cooking classes, and fitness centers offer demonstrations and nutrition seminars. Find a topic that relates to your business in some way and make it available to the public for free or for a nominal fee. If you don't want to present the information yourself, bring in an expert.

For Internet-based companies, you can hold online chats or a free conference call to discuss a topic. Visit www.FreeConferenceCall.com for a convenient service that can propel your business to exciting new levels of success.

Go the Extra Mile for Your Customer

Customer loyalty breeds valuable word-of-mouth marketing. But creating this kind of loyalty takes work. Think about it. What businesses are you loyal to? Would you return to a hair dresser you didn't like or who gave you a bad cut? Do you continue shopping at a local bakery because their products and services are superior, even though you could just pick something up at the grocery store?

One mortgage brokerage sends every one of its customers a copy of their closing statements at the end of the year. This saves each person from having to dig these papers up come tax time. Talk about a fantastic way to make your customers happy. This same broker sends each client a bottle of wine after a home loan is completed. This is a classy touch that the customers are bound to remember.

What can you do to create customer delight? You could send your clients a gift or pick up the phone to say, "Thank you for your business!" Don't forget about handwritten notes. With our reliance on e-mail today, it's always nice to receive a personally scribed note or card in the mail.

Cross Promote With Other Businesses

Start meeting business owners, whether in your town or across the Internet. Ask other businesses to hand out your coupon while you hand out theirs, or advertise in each other's newsletters or websites. Small business owners love to network with other business owners because we all share the same goal: to build a successful venture. Make sure you can offer something worthwhile in exchange instead of just asking for someone to help you.

Advertise in Local Newspapers or Magazines

This is one of the more expensive venues for promotion and only works well for certain types of businesses. Beware of offers that are less expensive because the ad placement is not ideal. Consider what publications and where in the publication your business should be seen. Advertising contacts are easily located in the publication's masthead or on their website. The smaller "neighborhood" newspapers are going to be far less expensive than the big town newspaper.

List in Membership Directories

If you are a member of a trade association, the chamber of commerce, Toastmasters or any organization, make sure you are listed in the membership directory along with a link and description of your business.

Pay-Per-Click

If you want to drive traffic to your website, pay-per-click is one of the hottest topics in Internet advertising. You can bid for placement in searches on Yahoo!, Google or other search engines based on key words that you specify. For example, you can indicate that if someone searches for "avocado trees," you are willing to pay $.XX per click through to your website. You decide how much you are willing to pay for each lead to your site, and the bids increase based on the popularity of the search term.

Many websites use this strategy, though it can become expensive when targeting popular key words. You might consider trying it out with just a few key words or try key word combinations that aren't as popular. Overture (www.Overture.com) is the most popular option for this service right now.

Trade Links

Your ongoing strategy should be to get your website link onto as many compatible sites as possible. Start by searching the Internet for key words that are complimentary to your business. For example, if you run an event planning business, you could search for hotels, tour companies, catering companies, and travel agents. Notice the sites that are listed in the top twenty—those are likely getting the most traffic for your industry.

Your next step is to evaluate these sites and see if there is an opportunity for you to trade links with the site operator. Some big sites won't be interested, but it never hurts to ask. You can send an e-mail directly to the owner and offer to swap links. If your site is new and growing, offer some extras to compensate for your lower traffic. You could offer to promote your partner's link in your newsletter for a full year, or place their link on the heading of your website.

Consider what you have to offer and make sure you present the site owner with a fair deal. Nobody wants to give away free advertising and the owner will probably try to sell you advertising instead of a link swap, so you must build a relationship and make it worth their while to work with you.

Advertising Vendors

There are some paid advertising venues that are available nationally and may work for your target audience if you have a brick and mortar business. Here are some vendors to investigate:

√ **The Welcome Wagon** (www.welcomewagon.com/) targets mailings to new home buyers. If this is your market, this could be a solution for you. The company sends out an address book to new home owners and says these books are usually kept for an average of five years.

√ **Valpak** (www.valpak.com) sends direct mail coupons in a blue envelope to neighborhoods of 10,000 people each month.

√ **The Penny Saver** (www.pennysaverusa.com/) is a free weekly newspaper that is mailed to homes and is packed full of classified ads and community resources. This may be a good place for a service business to advertise.

Additional Resources:

√ Jay Conrad Levinson has published dozens of *Guerrilla Marketing* books, teaching small business owners how to create powerful marketing strategies. Some titles to check out include *"Guerrilla Marketing: Secrets for Making Big Profits from Your Small Business," "Guerrilla Marketing in 30 Days,"* and *"Guerrilla Marketing for Free: Dozens of No-Cost Tactics to Promote Your Business and Energize Your Profits."* You can also visit Levinson's website and sign up for his free newsletter at www.gmarketing.com.

√ Joan Stewart's site, The Publicity Hound (www. publicity hound.com), is loaded with tips for getting free publicity and her newsletter won't disappoint.

√ The marketing section of Business Info Guide (www. BusinessInfoGuide.com/marketing) offers updated resources and marketing advice.

Entrepreneur Profile

Ida McCarty
Ida's Gourmet Breads
www.IdasGourmetBreads.com
Chicago, IL

After being downsized from her job as an IT Project Manager several times in a two-year period, Ida McCarty admits she fell into her business venture "by accident." She used a recipe from her grandmother and zucchini from her own garden to bake bread as a way to relieve stress.

In 2003, McCarty's then-fiancé (they later parted ways) approached a grocery store bakery manager and asked her to try the zucchini bread. McCarty says, "She ordered 100 loaves that week and has been a repeat customer ever since."

McCarty, who has a bachelor's degree in Political Science and a masters in Leadership and Policy Studies, never expected she would be baking bread for a living. She admits, "The business was started before I had an opportunity to think about baking bread as a career."

The journey into entrepreneurship meant that McCarty had a lot to learn—and fast. "I had to work backwards. I had a regular client so I had to take business classes, read material, network with other entrepreneurs while baking for my clients," says McCarty. "I had to bake out of a church kitchen until I established myself as a business six months later."

With a startup budget of $10,000, McCarty managed to come in under budget at $8,000, which she spent on licenses, supplies, and classes. She contacted vendors that sold her supplies in bulk quantities and found a caterer to rent her commercial kitchen *space on a monthly basis. To keep costs down, McCarty handles all her administrative tasks from home.*

Though her mother helps her with her baking, not all of her family and friends were as supportive from the beginning. "They felt as though I was baking as a hobby, as opposed to having a real job," says McCarty. "I had to prove to them that this was a real business venture."

This "real" venture has McCarty working an average of 60 hours per week to produce nine varieties of breads, including the zucchini that got her business started along with apple, carrot, banana, and gingerbread. "They are all preservative-free, no trans fats, no hydrogenated oils, high in fiber, and use only natural products. I grow the organic zucchini in my garden, freeze, and use it in my breads year-round."

To market her business, McCarty talks to retail bakery managers, gives product demonstrations, attends food fairs, participates in fundraisers, and submits articles to baking trade magazines.

Mentor Amy Hillard, the president of Comfort Cakes, provides McCarty with a tremendous amount of support. McCarty says, "She has taught me that perseverance wins out, professionalism shines through, and if you think small, you will remain small-minded."

Marge Schneider from The Service Corp of Retired Executives (SCORE) has also been instrumental in helping McCarty with her marketing strategy and product placement. SCORE is an organization that offers free assistance to entrepreneurs by helping them develop business plans and goals.

McCarty says her mother, Ida B. McCarty, "has been a Godsend in helping me aspire to a dream, reach my goals, bake and deliver my breads through rain, sleet, sun, and snow."

Though she had to knock on a lot of doors and take control of her future, McCarty says, "What I did not know, I found out by asking others." She admits that her busy work schedule leaves little room for a social life at this point, but it seems the trade-off has been worth it.

McCarty plans to have a full-time staff to handle baking, deliveries, and marketing within the next five years. She would like to market her breads to Fortune 500 companies and eventually sell the rights to a major corporation.

Her advice for aspiring entrepreneurs: "Don't think about it, just do it! Otherwise you will talk yourself out of taking a risk, languish in mediocrity, and always wonder what would have come of your dream and aspirations."

Her favorite online business resources include The Service Corp of Retired Executives (www.score.org), Women's Business Development Center (www.wbdc.org), The U.S. Small Business Administration (www.sba.gov), Business Matchmaking (www.businessmatchmaking.com), and Business Owners Idea Cafe (www.ideacafe.com).

As for her keys to success, McCarty says, "I never give up, never give in, and never take no for an answer." She is quite happy with her entrepreneurial life. "I control my own destiny. Success or failure is ultimately my own doing or undoing."

For now, McCarty is focused on getting her products into Whole Foods store locations across the mid-west region by the end of the year. The best part is that she no longer has to worry about being downsized from corporate America, while she enjoys the sweet smell of success.

> **Quick Tip**
>
> *Recognize employees for extra efforts or just to say thanks. Offer an afternoon off or a gift certificate to a local restaurant, coffee shop or movie theater.*

Chapter 14

Ready, Set, Go!

"Go confidently in the direction of your dreams.
Live the life you imagined."
–Henry David Thoreau

By now you should be well on your way to launching your business. Whether you plan to launch it part-time while maintaining your job, or you feel like you're ready to take a leap and go full-steam ahead, it's time to set a launch date. Pick a realistic date that gives you enough time to be fully prepared to turn on that "open" sign, whether it's a real neon sign or just an imaginary one in your home office. This is an important goal to specify and work toward. And don't worry if you fall behind— most business owners do! Just reset the date and keep moving forward.

Plan a Grand Opening Event

Whether you are working from your kitchen, an office building or a retail store front, a grand opening event is a great way to kick off your new business and build excitement around your offerings. Invite everyone you know: family, friends, neighbors, business associates, neighbors in your new building, the parents from your kid's school or Little League team—everyone! Make sure to send a press release to all local media alerting them to the big day.

You can pick up an inexpensive helium tank with balloons from a party supply store for less than $30. You could drop some cash on catering, or simply pick up several containers of cookies, treats, and punch.

You might want to offer door prizes or a special sale for the day. When I opened the bookstore, we put coupons in a grab bag and customers pulled out discounts ranging from 20% off their purchase to 50% off. We also had a few "Winner" coupons and gave away store t-shirts. Be creative and make it fun. Even if only two "real" customers show up, your family and friends should be happy to support you and it will be a day you will remember forever. Take some pictures that you can later use on your website or just to keep in a drawer for memories.

Revisit Your Business Plan

The first few months of business ownership will go by in a flash. Learn as you go, take notes, and solicit feedback from your clients. Don't let too much time go by without revisiting your business plan. Are you on target to meet the goals you set? Are your operating procedures working as planned? You will most likely need to make modifications.

Revisit and update your business plan quarterly. Set new goals as your business needs change and keep yourself accountable to those goals. Using your plan as a tool for success will give you a feeling of control over your environment and your bottom line. And you never know when you might need the plan down the road—when you decide to seek additional funding or bring in an investor. Imagine how impressed they will be when you whip out your updated plan without missing a beat.

Other Topics to Revisit Often

√ **Marketing** – Evaluate your marketing strategy and be open to new ideas. Vendors will find you so listen to what they have to offer. You can always say "no" but you might be intrigued by what they have to offer. If you can take one small action every day to market your business, you should build excellent momentum for business growth.

√ **Budget** – It is crucial to keep a close eye on your bottom line. Watch your spending closely and keep monthly track of your revenues, expenses and bank account balances. Lack of capital can ruin a business, so be sure to stick to your plans and address cash flow problems early.

√ **Customers** – Get to know your customers and listen to them. Ask them for feedback and make sure you are providing exceptional customer service. It is easy to get caught up in the nuts and bolts of running a business and lose perspective of the most important areas of focus. Your customers are crucial to your success and should be considered in everything that you do.

√ **Education** – Keep an eye on your industry, the economy, and business climate in general. Read the business news and visit the bookstore often for new books that will help you keep a fresh perspective on running your business. Education is power!

Final Thoughts

You don't have to feel like you are alone in your entrepreneurial endeavors. I encourage you to use your networks and create a support system. You can not only learn from your peers, but you can find a tremendous amount of support from them.

You shouldn't rush into anything when it comes to starting a business. It is wonderful to have enthusiasm—just be careful that it doesn't take over and cause you to make decisions that you might later regret.

Most importantly—*enjoy the ride.* Launching a business is unlike anything you have ever done before and you shouldn't be riddled with anxiety, especially if you have taken the time to prepare.

Let Me Know How You're Doing

I want to hear from readers so I can continue to provide you, my customers, with valuable information. Perhaps your business venture could be a future entrepreneur success story in one of my books! Send your comments and suggestions to: BookFee dback@BusinessInfoGuide.com. Good luck with all of your business ventures!

Appendix

Book Suggestions

To be truly successful in business, you must keep learning. Books provide an easy and affordable way to discover new ideas and continue your education while you build and grow your business. The following are some of my personal favorites:

√ *"Guerrilla Marketing Weapons: 100 Affordable Marketing Methods for Maximizing Profits from Your Small Business"* (and any of the *Guerrilla Marketing* books—they're fabulous) by Jay Conrad Levinson

√ *"If Success Is a Game, These Are the Rules: Ten Rules for a Fulfilling Life"* by Cherie Carter-Scott

√ *"301 Do-It-Yourself Marketing Ideas: From America's Most Innovative Small Companies"* by Sam Decker

√ *"301 Great Management Ideas from America's Most Innovative Small Companies"* by Sara P. Noble

√ *"Zero to Six Figures"* by Jennifer Keenan Bonoff

√ *"The Street Smart Entrepreneur: 133 Tough Lessons I Learned the Hard Way"* by Jay Goltz and Jody Oesterreicher

√ *"What No One Ever Tells You About Starting Your Own Business: Real Life Start-Up Advice from 101 Successful Entrepreneurs"* by Jan Norman

√ *"Mastering the Art of Selling"* by Tom Hopkins

√ *"Making a Living Without a Job: Winning Ways for Creating Work That You Love"* by Barbara Winter

√ *"Kick Start Your Dream Business: Getting it Started and Keeping You Going"* by Romanus Wolter

Magazines

These small business magazines can be found at most newsstands and all have companion websites.

√ *Entrepreneur* – www.Entrepreneur.com
√ *Inc.* – www.INC.com
√ *Fortune Small Business (FSB)* – www.Fortunesb.com
√ *Fast Company* – www.FastCompany.com
√ *Small Business Opportunities* – www.SBOmag.com
√ *Black Enterprise* – www.BlackEnterprise.com
√ *Home Business Magazine* – www.HomeBusinessMag.com
√ *American Venture* – www.avce.com
√ *Business 2.0* – www.Business2.com

Small Business Websites

Make sure to add these sites to your favorite resources for additional information.

√ **Business Info Guide** provides free resources and industry information for entrepreneurs including a printable business startup checklist, articles by experts, and a monthly newsletter loaded with hot tips. www.BusinessInfoGuide.com
√ The **U.S. Small Business Administration** offers free business planning tools. www.sba.gov
√ The **Service Corp of Retired Executives** provides free business consulting services. www.SCORE.org
√ **Business Owner's Idea Cafe** is a unique resource for more free business advice. This site offers free message boards where you can exchange information with other business owners, lists available business grants, trade magazines and planning tools. www.IdeaCafe.com
√ The **Wall Street Journal's** website for entrepreneurs includes articles and tips for small business and franchising. www. StartupJournal.com

Small Business Solutions

There are hundreds of companies that offer various packages for business so this list only represents a small fraction of your options. Be sure to shop around and find the best solutions for your business needs and budget.

√ **Yahoo!** offers website hosting, domain registration, marketing services, storefront on their shopping channel and other services. www.SmallBusiness.Yahoo.com

√ **PayPal** is owned by auction giant eBay and offers comprehensive online payment services and even free shopping cart software. www.PayPal.com

√ **1ShoppingCart** offers a comprehensive package of solutions including shopping cart software, merchant card processing, establishing your own affiliate account, auto-responders for e-mail management, and e-book distribution tools. www.1Shoppingcart.com.

√ Businesses can buy and sell items on **eBay** and use the auction site to liquidate excess inventory. EBay also has a storefront program for those interested in an ongoing presence on the site. www.eBay.com

√ **The Ultimate Trade Show Network** website lists trade shows all over the country. www.tsnn.com/

About the Author

Stephanie Chandler is a small business advisor, owner of Book Lovers Bookstore in Sacramento and BusinessInfoGuide.com, a directory of free resources for entrepreneurs. She is also a skilled public speaker and has published hundreds of business articles in a variety of publications.

After spending more than a decade in the Silicon Valley, Chandler fled her career in software sales to pursue her entrepreneurial and writing goals. She was inspired to launch BusinessInfoGuide.com and write this book out of frustration when starting her first business. She found it difficult to locate the information she needed even though she read dozens of business books. Her goal is to make it easier for others to follow their entrepreneurial dreams.

Chandler resides in Northern California with her husband (a patient man who makes her laugh every day), stepson, one-eyed cat, and an intellectually challenged rescue-mutt named "Mojo." She can be reached via e-mail at Stephanie@BusinessInfoGuid e.com.

Secure Order Form

Check Your Local Bookstore or Order Here

Please send me _____ copies of The Business Startup Checklist at $15.95 each, plus $3.50 shipping for the first book, $1.99 for each additional book. California residents, please add $1.16 sales tax per book. International orders must be paid by money order in US funds and shipping fees increased to $7.00 per book. Quantity discounts are available—please contact us for more information.

My check or money order for a total of $_____ is enclosed OR....
Please charge my Visa or Mastercard #_____
Name as it appears on card:_____
Expiration date:_____
Signature:_____

Shipping Information:

Name_____
Organization/Business_____
Address_____
City/State/Zip_____
Phone_____ E-mail_____

Please make your check payable and mail with completed order form to:
Book Lovers Bookstore
5800 Madison Ave, Suite W
Sacramento, CA 95670

Order online at: www.BusinessInfoGuide.com

Index

Printed in the United States
38405LVS00002B/76